Lernkrimi Englisch

Blood and Breakfast

Andrew Ridley
Alison Romer

compact

Weitere Informationen zu Compact Lernkrimis finden Sie am Ende des Buches und unter www.lernkrimi.de.

Baierbrunner Straße 27, 81379 München
Ausgabe 2014
12. Auflage

Chefredaktion: Dr. Matthias Feldbaum
Redaktion: Helga Aichele
Fachkorrektur: Fiona Cain
Produktion: Ute Hausleiter
Titelillustration: Karl Knospe
Lernkrimi-Logo: Carsten Abelbeck
Gestaltung: Maria Seidel
Umschlaggestaltung: EKH Werbeagentur GbR, Hartmut Baier

ISBN 978-3-8174-7760-9
7277605/12

www.compactverlag.de, www.lernkrimi.de

Vorwort

Mit den neuen, spannenden Compact Kurzkrimis können Sie Ihre Englischkenntnisse auf schnelle und einfache Weise vertiefen, auffrischen und überprüfen.
Die vier fesselnden Kurzkrimis sind ideal für geübte Anfänger und Wiedereinsteiger.
Jeder Krimi wird durch abwechslungsreiche und kurzweilige Übungen ergänzt, die das Lernen unterhaltsam und spannend machen. Prüfen Sie Ihr Englisch in Lückentexten, Zuordnungs- und Übersetzungsaufgaben, in Buchstabenspielen und Kreuzworträtseln!
Ob im Bus oder in der Bahn, im Wartezimmer, zu Hause oder in der Mittagspause – das Sprachtraining im handlichen Format bietet die ideale Trainingsmöglichkeit für zwischendurch.
Schreiben Sie die Lösungen einfach ins Buch!
Die richtigen Antworten sind in einem eigenen Lösungsteil am Ende des Buches zusammengefasst. Im Anhang befindet sich außerdem ein Glossar, in dem die schwierigsten Wörter übersetzt sind. Diese sind im Text kursiv markiert.

Und nun kann die Spannung beginnen ...

Viel Spaß und Erfolg!

Inhalt

Blood and Breakfast 5
Stolen Summer 37
Death Wish 70
Motive for Murder 103
Abschlusstest 136
Lösungen 142
Glossar 146

Blood and Breakfast

Inspector Rush macht Ferien in Kent. Ein nächtlicher Schuss weckt seine Ermittlerinstinkte: Haben Wilderer geschossen oder gehen in dem Bed & Breakfast ganz andere Dinge vor?

Stolen Summer

In einem Dorf in Lancashire werden Gemälde eines lokalen Künstlers gestohlen. Sergeant Rose tappt zunächst im Dunkeln, aber dann weisen die Bilder selbst auf das Motiv hin ...

Death Wish

Seit einiger Zeit erhält Phillip Hanson Drohbriefe. Die Polizei scheint der Sache zunächst kaum Beachtung zu schenken, doch dann wird aus den Drohungen blutiger Ernst ...

Motive for Murder

Wurde die erfolgreiche Nachrichtensprecherin Tessa wirklich von ihrem Liebhaber ermordet? Ihre Schwester Clea glaubt an seine Unschuld und macht sich selbst auf die Suche nach dem Täter. Schon bald stößt sie auf eine heiße Spur ...

BLOOD AND BREAKFAST

Andrew Ridley

Chapter 1: A Shot in the Night

How good it is to be on holiday with my daughter, thinks Detective Inspector Rush. He is happy to be away from his job in Leeds in the north of England for a few days. His job is very important to him, but he also likes to spend time with his daughter, Sally. A week in Kent on the south east coast will be *enjoyable* for both of them.

"Drive a little slower, Dad," says Sally. "You aren't driving a police car now. I would like to enjoy the *view*. It's so beautiful."

They are driving along the coast road between Folkestone and Hastings and there is a beautiful *view* of the sea.

"Okay," says her father. "We have a few hours yet. We must arrive in time for the evening meal, though."

They are quiet for a few minutes, and then he speaks again.

"I'm so *pleased* that you have come on holiday with me," he says. "There are not many 24-year-old daughters who want to go on holiday with their fathers."

"No," she laughs. "You really are very lucky to have me with you."

He laughs as well. "Yes, I know I am. It's so long since we spent some time together. I think that the last time was two years ago, when we went on the Aikido course in Birmingham. I'm sorry that I always seem to be so *busy*."

"Don't *worry* about it, Dad," she replies. "It makes the time that we do spend together really special."

"Thanks," he answers. "I'm really looking forward to this week. *Especially* the open-air classical concert at Leeds Castle. That should be really good."

"Yes," she agrees. "The 1812 Overture with real cannons and fireworks should be *amazing*."
After a moment, she asks, "Do you know why it's called Leeds Castle? It can't be anything to do with the city of Leeds where we live, can it?"
"No," replies her father, "it isn't. I read somewhere that the Saxons called the area 'Esledes'. Over the years it became 'Leeds'."
"You're so clever, Dad," says Sally, *proudly*. "Sometimes I think that you know everything."
Detective Inspector Rush smiles, but says nothing.
Sally looks at her father. He is 47 years old, but he looks younger. His brown hair has some grey at the sides. He is not *handsome*, she thinks, but he is good-looking. He is also still a fit man. They used to do Aikido together, but now her father practises yoga.

! ÜBUNG 1

Übung 1: Trifft die Aussage zu?
Markieren Sie mit richtig ✔ oder falsch – !

1. Sally's father is a policeman in the north of England. ☐
2. Sally and her father are going on holiday to Kent. ☐
3. They are travelling by bus. ☐
4. They will go to a rock concert at Leeds Castle. ☐
5. DI Rush is old and ugly. ☐
6. He does not spend a lot of time with his daughter. ☐
7. Sally and her father do yoga together. ☐
8. Leeds Castle is in the city of Leeds. ☐

Twenty minutes later they drive past St Mary's *Bay* and after a few hundred metres see a sign at the side of the road.
"Littlestone Farm, Bed and Breakfast," reads Sally. "That's it."

DI Rush turns left down a narrow lane. He drives slowly, as the road is *uneven*. After a few minutes they arrive in the *yard* of a small farm. There is a house with a *thatched* roof and a *barn* stands at the end of the *yard*. DI Rush parks his car at the side of it. They both climb out of the car and *stretch*. A dog is barking and as they turn towards the house, the door opens. A man dressed in old jeans and a dirty, blue shirt stands in the *doorway*. He is about forty years old, small and *wiry* with brown hair. As they *approach*, Sally can see that his eyes are a beautiful blue.

"Good afternoon," he says. "Mr Rush, is it?" He holds out a *grubby* hand. "I'm Alan, Alan Larkin." They *shake* hands. "And you must be Sally," he says as he turns towards her. She *shakes* his hand *reluctantly*, because she doesn't like the fact that it is dirty.

"Come inside," he says. "Brenda will make you a cup of tea and then you can bring in your cases and *unpack*." They follow him into the house. "How was your journey here?" he asks. He doesn't wait for an answer, but calls, "Brenda, Mr Rush and his daughter are here."

DI Rush and Sally walk behind him down the *hall* and into the living room. There are two large *settees*, a television, a dining table with six chairs and other pieces of furniture. Sally is *surprised* to see that the room is clean and *tidy*. Not like Mr Larkin, she thinks. Brenda *appears* from the kitchen. She looks a little older than Mr Larkin and is also a few inches taller. She is quite large and has a round face with red cheeks. She wipes her hands on a towel before she *shakes* their hands.

"I'm just making the evening meal," she says. "I hope you like meat and potato pie."

"Yes, that will be fine, Mrs Larkin," says DI Rush. "Sally used to be a *vegetarian*, but she started to eat meat again last year."

"Please call me Brenda, Mr Rush," she says. "Well, I'm sure you'll

enjoy my pie, Sally. Everyone does. Now sit down and I'll bring you both a nice cup of tea. You must be ready for a drink after driving all that way."
She goes back into the kitchen and Mr Larkin follows her.

I wish that my mother and father were still together, thinks Sally. DI Rush has been in the police for twenty-five years. Twelve years ago he became a detective inspector, and two years later her mother left him because he was never at home. He was always working. Since then, Sally has lived with her mother. I love them both, she thinks. Sometimes life is so difficult.

They sit on the *settee* and look around at the pictures on the walls.
"What do you think so far?" asks the inspector.
"Well, it's not The Ritz, but it seems okay," replies Sally. "Mr Larkin looks a bit *grubby,* though. I'm glad he's not cooking our evening meal."
They both laugh.
Just then Mr Larkin comes through the kitchen door. Behind him is Mrs Larkin with a *tray* in her hands. She places the cups and teapot on the table.
"Did you have a good journey here?" she asks as she *pours* the tea.
"Yes, thank you," answers DI Rush, as unlike Mr Larkin, Mrs Larkin waits for an answer.
When they all have a cup of tea, Mr Larkin asks, "What job do you do, Mr Rush?"
"Please, call me David," replies DI Rush. "I work in a bank, the same as Sally," he lies. When he is on holiday, he never tells people that he is a policeman. People always want to talk about police work or *complain* about the police. "Is this actually a farm or do you just have the bed and breakfast business?" he asks.

"The only animal we have here is a dog," replies Mrs Larkin. "I *run* the bed and breakfast. Alan has a large *van*. He carries things about for people. It brings in a little extra money."

"What kind of dog do you have?" asks Sally. "I like dogs."

"I don't think you would like Brutus," says Mrs Larkin. "He's a large Rottweiler and he's not very friendly. We keep him locked in the backyard when we have visitors."

They continue talking until they have finished their tea. Then Mr Larkin helps DI Rush to bring in the suitcases from the car. He takes them up to their rooms. Both rooms are at the front of the house and look out onto the *yard*. In each room is a single bed, a wardrobe with *drawers* and a chair. Each room also has an *en suite* bathroom with a shower.

"If you want to go for a walk before dinner, the beach is not far from here," says Mr Larkin. "If you go down the path between the house and the *barn,* you'll arrive at the sea in twenty minutes."

"Thanks," answers DI Rush. "It would be nice to go for a walk. My legs are stiff after the journey from Leeds."

Übung 2: Beantworten Sie die Fragen zum Text!

ÜBUNG 2 !

1. How have Sally and her father travelled to Kent?

____

2. Why does Sally shake Mr Larkin's hand reluctantly?

____

3. Who comes out of the kitchen?

____

4. Where does DI Rush say that he works?

5. What is Mrs Larkin doing in the kitchen?

6. Who is Brutus?

DI Rush *unpacks* his case and hangs his clothes in the old, wooden wardrobe. After a hot shower, he feels *refreshed*. When he has dressed in blue jeans, a blue *short-sleeved* shirt and a *leather* jacket, he knocks on Sally's door. She is still in the shower, however. Just like her mother, he thinks to himself and smiles. She used to take hours to get herself ready to go out. He goes down into the living room to wait for her.

He looks up from the newspaper that he is reading when Sally *eventually* comes down the stairs. She is also wearing blue jeans, but she has on a yellow T-shirt. Her long, blonde hair is *tied* back in a *ponytail*.

"Are you sure that you'll be warm enough?" asks her father. "It may be windy down by the sea."

"Of course I'll be warm enough, Dad. You *worry* too much," she laughs.

They leave the house and follow the path between the house and the *barn*. It goes through fields and a small wood. When they come out of the wood they can see the sea.

"Oh, the *English Channel,*" says Sally. "Can you see France?"

"I can see something," replies her father, "but it's probably just a low cloud."

They walk on in the evening sunlight to the top of the cliff. Then they stop for a moment to look at the sea and watch the large ships out on the water.

"Shall we go down to the beach?" asks Sally and begins to go down the *steep* path. DI Rush follows her *carefully*.

"Not too fast," he calls. "My legs are older than yours."

They spend some time on the beach, where they walk by the sea and throw *pebbles* into the water. Then they climb back up the path.

"You're very quiet, Dad," says Sally. "Is anything the matter?"

"Not really," he replies. "I was just thinking that the path from the farm is very easy to follow. It looks as though lots of people use it. I think that's *strange* when there are only a few guests each week."

He bends and picks up a cigarette packet from the ground.

"French cigarettes," he says. "Perhaps they have had French guests."

"Really, Dad," laughs Sally. "Don't you ever stop being a detective? I have a friend who smokes Russian cigarettes and she's not Russian."

They make their way back to the farm and as they enter the *yard*, they see that a large, new BMW is parked in front of the *barn*. As they go into the house, Mrs Larkin is serving the evening meal. There is already a man sitting at the dining table.

"Hello, you two," calls Mrs Larkin. "You're *just in time*. This is Mr Dalton. He's staying here for the night."

DI Rush and Sally introduce themselves to Mr Dalton. He is about thirty years of age, *slim* and has short, blonde hair. He is dressed in an expensive suit, and the inspector sees that he has a Rolex watch on his *wrist*.

Sally thinks he is quite good-looking and during the meal, she tries to talk to him. Mr Dalton, however, doesn't want to talk. He answers her questions with "yes" or "no" and *eventually* she gives up and talks to her father instead.

After the meal, Mr Dalton goes upstairs to his room. Mrs Larkin *clears the table* and returns to the kitchen.
"Mr Dalton doesn't say very much, does he?" says Sally when they are alone.
"No," replies her father. "He didn't want to talk about himself, did he? I *wonder* what his job is. That was a very expensive Rolex that he had on his *wrist,* and new BMWs aren't cheap."
"Well, I don't think we're going to find out," says Sally. "Mrs Larkin said that he's only here for one night."
They sit on the *settee*. Sally watches the television and DI Rush reads a book that he has brought with him.

ÜBUNG 3 !

Übung 3: Welches Wort ist das „schwarze Schaf"?
Unterstreichen Sie das nicht in die Reihe passende Wort!

1. our, week, month, minute
2. settee, dining table, chair, furniture
3. daughter, friend, father, mother
4. hand, eye, pie, cheek
5. shirt, case, jacket, jeans
6. wardrobe, bed, drawer, yard
7. beach, pebbles, settee, water
8. Rolex, yard, barn, field

At 9 p.m. Mrs Larkin makes a cup of tea for them, and at 10 p.m. they decide to go to bed. They are both tired after the journey.
DI Rush lies awake for a little while. He thinks about what they will do in the morning. He also thinks about Mr Dalton. Why is a man with so much money at a bed and breakfast? He should be in a four-star hotel, thinks DI Rush as he falls asleep.

It is still dark when he suddenly *wakes up*. He is sure that the noise that *woke* him was a *gunshot*. He *switches on* the lamp at the side of his bed and looks at the clock. Half past three. He *switches off* the lamp again and gets out of bed. He looks out of his window, but the *yard* below is completely black. Since he is awake, he decides to get up and have a look outside. He puts on his trousers, shoes and a jumper and quietly goes down the stairs. He unlocks and opens the front door.

Suddenly, the light in the *hall* is *switched on*.

"It's a little early to be going out for a walk, isn't it, Mr Rush?" says a voice behind him.

DI Rush's heart is *beating* like a *drum*. He turns and sees that Mr Larkin has come out of the living room. Behind him stands a large, black Rottweiler. The dog *growls* deeply when DI Rush looks at it.

"Be quiet, Brutus!" says Larkin.

The dog stops *growling,* but it doesn't take its eyes off DI Rush.

"Something *woke* me," says the detective. "It sounded like a *gun-shot*."

"Yes, I heard it, too," says Mr Larkin. "I was in the living room. I must have fallen asleep while I was watching the television."

"What do you think it was?" asks the DI.

"It's probably *poachers*," replies Larkin. "They are often around here at night. Don't go out when they *are about.* You could be *injured* or even killed. You wouldn't be the first person to be killed by a *poacher's bullet*."

"No," he replies. "You're probably right. I think I'll go back to bed and see if I can sleep."

DI Rush starts to climb the stairs and then turns to look back. Mr Larkin has returned to the *lounge*, but Brutus is standing there watching him with cold, black eyes.

Chapter 2: Blood on the Ground

At breakfast that morning, only Sally and her father are at the table. "Where's Mr Dalton?" asks Sally when Mrs Larkin comes from the kitchen.

"Oh, he was up very early," she replies. "He had to catch a *ferry* to France. He needed to be in Paris for a meeting this morning."

"Why didn't he fly?" asks the inspector.

"He needed his car with him," replies Mrs Larkin quickly and her cheeks begin to *redden*. "Now, what can I get you for breakfast?"

"A full English breakfast for me," says the inspector. "Could I have a *fried egg*, please?"

"And for me, two *poached* eggs on toast, please," says Sally.

ÜBUNG 4 !

Übung 4: Lesen Sie weiter und unterstreichen Sie im folgenden Abschnitt die richtige Übersetzung der Wörter in Klammern!
(1. Küche, 2. Fähre, 3. Zug, 4. Hof, 5. Schuss, 6. Nacht)

When Mrs Larkin returns to the kitchen, they both look at each other.

"It's *strange* that Mr Dalton left so early for the *ferry*. If he needed his car in Paris, he could have gone on the Eurotunnel train with it," says the inspector.

"Perhaps he likes to drive," Sally replies. "He left early. I heard his car in the *yard* when it was still dark. It *woke* me."

"I didn't hear that," says her father, "but I did hear something else." He then tells her about the shot that he heard in the night.

"Really?" *gasps* Sally. "You don't think that had anything to do with Mr Dalton leaving early, do you?"

"I hope not," answers her father.
"And Mr Larkin said it was *poachers*?" Sally continues. "That's terrible. I hate to think that people go around with *guns* and kill poor animals in the middle of the night. The world would be a better place without *guns*."
They stop talking as Mrs Larkin returns from the kitchen. She places a plate in front of the inspector.
"Here's your full English breakfast, David," she says. "And here are your *poached* eggs on toast, Sally. I hope they're not too hard," she *adds*, as she puts a plate in front of Sally.
"That smells delicious," says the inspector, as he looks at his plate full of food: two eggs, bacon, *mushrooms*, beans and fried bread. "I'll need a long walk after this," he continues. "After a week here, I'll be fat. Your cooking is really excellent, Brenda."
She smiles and goes back into the kitchen.
A few seconds later she *appears* again with a pot of tea. She places it on the table and then leaves them alone.
DI Rush and Sally eat their breakfast. They discuss how they will spend their day. It is a beautiful morning with a blue sky and warm sunshine. They decide to visit Canterbury, as they have never been there. They would both like to see the famous cathedral.
When Mrs Larkin returns to *clear the table*, they talk with her about Canterbury. Finally, DI Rush asks where Mr Larkin is.
"He had to leave early as well," she replies. "He's gone up to London to see someone about some business."
Before he can ask anything else, Mrs Larkin hurries off into the kitchen.

Sally and her father go upstairs to their rooms and pack a small rucksack each. Sally goes out into the *yard* and sees her father near the *barn* door. As she walks towards him, she slips. She looks down

and sees a small *pool* of red *liquid*. She bends down to look at it and her father comes over to her.
"What is it, Dad?" she asks. "It looks like blood to me."
Her father puts his finger into the *liquid* and *examines* it. "I think you're right," he says. "What's a *pool* of blood doing here in the *yard*?"
"Brutus caught a *rabbit* this morning and brought it into the *yard*," says Mrs Larkin. She is standing behind them with a bucket of water. "I'm sorry that you had to see that," she continues. "I was going to clean it up earlier, but I was *busy* in the kitchen." She *pours* the water onto the blood to wash it away. When she is happy that all of the blood has *disappeared*, she goes back into the house. Sally and her father stand in *silence*. They look at each other and he *shrugs his shoulders*.
"I thought they locked Brutus in the back *yard*," Sally says.
"That's what Mrs Larkin said yesterday," agrees her father. "Perhaps the *poachers* are not the only killers around here *after dark*. I don't like to think that Brutus is walking about freely at night."
"Oh, don't think about it, then," says Sally. "Let's go and have a nice day in Canterbury."

! ÜBUNG 5

Übung 5: Wie heißt der Begriff auf Englisch? Übersetzen Sie!

1. Spiegelei ____________________
2. Pilz ____________________
3. hinzufügen ____________________
4. Gewehr ____________________
5. Tablett ____________________

6. sich beklagen ______________________

7. ordentlich ______________________

They spend a *pleasant* day in Canterbury. They visit the castle and the cathedral, and they have lunch at one of the cafés in the town centre. They also look around the shops before they return to their car and drive back to Littlestone Farm.

On their return, Mr Larkin is standing at the door of the house.
"Did you have a good time in Canterbury?" he asks.
"Yes we did, thanks," replies DI Rush. "How was London?"
"Too *busy* and too noisy," Larkin laughs.
"Did you drive there?" asks the DI.
"Yes," Larkin answers *cautiously*. "Why?"
"It's just that your *van* was still in the *barn* this morning," answers the DI.
The smile *disappears* from Larkin's face and his cold, blue eyes turn towards DI Rush. "I walked to the end of the lane and a friend took me in his car," he says after a moment.
"Oh, right," replies DI Rush.
"Any more questions?" he asks *sharply*.
"No, Alan," answers the inspector. "None at all."
Larkin turns and *disappears* into the house.
Sally and the inspector look at each other before they follow him through the door. They go upstairs to their rooms to wash before the evening meal.
Tonight they are the only two at the table. While they eat, Sally and the inspector discuss their day in Canterbury, but both of them are thinking about the *strange* things that have happened since they arrived at Littlestone Farm. Mrs Larkin serves their food but doesn't say much this evening. Mr Larkin is nowhere to be seen.

After the meal, Sally watches TV again while her father reads his book. When they go upstairs, they both go into Sally's room.
"Something's not right here," says DI Rush, after she has closed the door. "I think I'll stay awake tonight and see if anything happens."
"Oh, Dad," says Sally. "You're not at work now. Just go to bed."
"Sorry, Sally," he replies. "I have a *suspicious* mind. I just want to see if anything happens during the night here."
"Well, be *careful*, Dad," Sally warns. "There are *obviously* people out there at night with *guns*."
"Don't *worry*. I can take care of myself," says her father, before he goes to his room. He takes off his shoes and lies on the bed. He *sets* his alarm clock for 2 a.m. and then closes his eyes.

He only seems to have slept for seconds when the alarm *wakes* him. After he stops the alarm, he lies for a few minutes on the bed. Then he gets up, goes to the open window and looks out. The *yard* is completely dark and there is no sound at all. He sits by the window and the hours go by. The only sounds he hears are a dog barking somewhere and also an *owl* in the wood. When it starts to become light, he undresses and gets into bed, where he soon falls asleep.

! ÜBUNG 6

Übung 6: Lesen Sie weiter und setzen Sie das richtige Wort ein!
(everyone, breakfast, enjoy, laughs, agrees, suspicious, father, beautiful)

At (1.) ______________ the next morning, he tells Sally about his night.

"Perhaps you are too (2.) ______________, Dad," she says. "I think it's the fact that you're a policeman that makes you *suspect* (3.)

______________. Don't you think?"

"You could be right," her father (4.) ______________. "I think that I should leave my work behind for a week and just (5.) ______________ my holiday. The weather is (6.) ______________ and the food is great."

"And, of course, the *company* is wonderful," Sally *adds* and she (7.) ______________.

"Indeed it is," agrees her (8.) ______________ and he laughs, too.

They spend the day in Ramsgate on the coast. It is some distance away, but DI Rush had a holiday there when he was a teenager and wants to go back. He finds that he cannot really *remember* much. Everything is more modern now. However, they have a *pleasant* day. They do all the things that DI Rush used to do when he was a teenager on holiday. They walk by the sea, eat fish and chips and go to the *fairground*. They go on the rides and at one of the *stalls*, DI Rush wins a *bar* of chocolate by throwing *darts*. They have both eaten enough, so he puts it in his pocket for later.

For Sally it is a new *experience*. She has spent all her holidays in Spain or France. She has never had a holiday on the coast in England. When they arrive back at Littlestone Farm, Mr Larkin is in the *barn*. The doors are open and they can see him in the back of his *van*. He has a bucket and a *cloth*. He looks up as they get out of the car. They are both laughing.

"You've *obviously* had a good day," he says. "It must be nice to have no work to do."

"It is very nice indeed," replies DI Rush. "Are you going out with the *van* this evening, Alan?"

"No," Larkin answers *sharply*. "I just thought that I should clean it out. Then it will be ready when I need it again."
He turns away and begins to clean the floor.
DI Rush looks at Sally and *shrugs his shoulders*. They walk across the *yard* and into the house. Mrs Larkin is *obviously* in the kitchen and the smell of the evening meal fills the *hall*.
"It smells like *roast* lamb," says Sally. "The meals here really are delicious."
"I can hardly *believe* that you used to be a *vegetarian*," her father laughs.

! ÜBUNG 7

Übung 7: Lesen Sie weiter und unterstreichen Sie alle 14 Verben im folgenden Abschnitt!

Apparently, they are still the only guests at the house. While they eat their evening meal, they talk together. They also speak to Mrs Larkin when she *appears* from the kitchen to serve the food. They tell her about their visit to Ramsgate and DI Rush's holiday there years ago. When they have eaten, they decide to sit in the garden to drink their coffee. It is a beautiful evening and they watch the sun *disappear* behind the wood.

"Two days gone already," says Sally. "I can't *believe* how quickly the time goes by."
"Yes, it will soon be time to pack our cases," replies her father.
"Well, Mrs Larkin is okay and I really like her meals," says Sally, "but I'm not sure about Mr Larkin. Sometimes I think he is okay and at other times I feel that there's something *suspicious* about him."
"I think that we both agree on that," the inspector laughs. Then he continues more *seriously*. "You know what I said this morning,

about forgetting police work for a week. Well, I still think Mr Larkin is doing something illegal. I think I might stay awake again tonight."

"Well, I think that you should go to sleep tonight. You have been *yawning* all day today," says Sally.

They go inside and watch television together for an hour. Then they go up to their rooms.

"Are you really going to stay awake tonight, Dad?" Sally asks, as she goes into her room.

"I don't know," replies her father. "As you said, I should really sleep tonight. I might *set* my alarm and just get up for a short time to see if anything is happening."

Sally smiles. She knows that her father will get up during the night. He has been a detective for too many years now. If he thinks there is something *suspicious* going on, then he will not be able to get a good night's sleep.

"Goodnight, Dad," she smiles. "Sleep well."

Übung 8: Lesen Sie weiter und finden Sie die Synonyme für die folgenden Ausdrücke im Text!

(1. half an hour, 2. noises, 3. night bird, 4. return, 5. silent, 6. farm building, 7. vehicle, 8. short moments of time, 9. it is likely that)

! ÜBUNG 8

At 2 a.m. DI Rush is waiting by his open window. He sits there for thirty minutes, and once again the only sounds that he hears are the barking of the dog and the call of the *owl*. He is about to go back to bed when he hears someone *swear* quietly. He puts his head out of the window, but everything is quiet again. With his head out of the window, he can see that there is a light on in the *barn*. Perhaps Larkin is working on his *van*, he thinks. However, there is no sound at all. He thinks for a few seconds and then decides to go and see what is happening in the *barn*. Probably Larkin didn't *switch* the light *off*, the inspector tells himself.

He goes quietly down the stairs. The house is dark and silent. He is just about to open the door and go out into the *yard* when he hears a deep *growl* behind him. The hair on the back of his neck stands up. The inspector does not move his body but slowly turns his head. In the darkness he can see the *shape* of Brutus. The Rottweiler is standing in the *hall* behind him. Brutus *growls* again and takes a step towards him.

"Good dog," says the inspector quietly. "Nice dog."

Although it is dark, he can see that the dog is ready to jump at him. He puts his hand in his pocket to see if he has anything to *protect* himself with. His fingers *touch* the *bar* of chocolate that he won at the *fairground*. Quickly, he breaks a piece from the *bar* and throws it to the dog.

"Good dog, do you like chocolate?" he says.

In the darkness, he can see the dog take the chocolate from the floor and *swallow* it quickly. His hand is *trembling* as he throws another piece to it, and then another. While the dog is eating the chocolate, DI Rush opens the door and escapes into the *yard*. He quickly closes the door behind him and stands still for a moment. He *breathes* deeply and waits a few minutes until his heart is *beating* more slowly.

Perhaps I should have stayed in bed, he tells himself. How can I go back into the house now? Brutus will be waiting for me. If there is nothing in the *barn*, I will have to sleep in there until the Larkins get up. And then I will have to *explain* why I was out in the *yard* in the middle of the night.

Nevertheless, DI Rush wants to find out what goes on in the *barn*.

Übung 9: Lesen Sie weiter und ordnen Sie die Buchstaben in Klammern zu einem sinnvollen Wort!

In the (1. dary) ____________ there is only his car. The (2. thilg) ____________ is still on in the *barn*. He stands for a (3. tenomm) ____________ and listens. He can now (4. erah) ____________ noises which come from the *barn*. It sounds like voices – like someone talking, but very (5. elyquit) ____________.

He walks across the *yard* and goes to the side of the *barn*, where there is a (6. nowwid) ____________. With his hand he cleans the years of dirt from the glass until it is (7. encreal) ____________ and he can see through it. Then, he puts his face (8. stagina) ____________ the window and looks into the *barn*.

At first he can only see Larkin's *van*. Then he sees someone moving in the corner of the *barn*. As they walk into the light, he *gasps*.

"So that's Larkin's secret," he says to himself and he takes out his mobile phone to call the police. At that moment, he hears a deep *growl* behind him. Before he can do anything, something hits him on the back of the head and he falls to the ground *unconscious*.

Chapter 3: Death Waits at the Bedroom Door

Up in her room, Sally cannot sleep. Perhaps it is the cheese that she ate at the evening meal. She *wakes up* several times and lies in bed listening to the *owl* in the wood. Then she hears a sound on the stairs.

Sally's heart begins to *beat* faster. She climbs out of bed and slowly and quietly opens her door. She sees her father going *carefully* down the stairs and into the *hall*. She does not want to speak, as she might *wake* the Larkins. She gently closes her door again and sits on the bed.

What should I do, she thinks to herself. What has Dad seen? Should I follow him or should I stay in my room? Finally, Sally decides to get dressed but to stay in her room and wait to see if anything happens.

Dressed in jeans and a jumper, she sits by her window and looks out onto the dark, silent *yard*. The night air is cool and she is glad that she has put on a jumper.

After a few moments she hears the front door open. It is then gently closed, and she sees a figure *cautiously* cross the *yard* towards the *barn*. She is sure that it is her father. But what has he been doing downstairs? It has taken him a long time to leave the house. The figure goes down the side of the *barn* and *disappears* from her *view*.

Sally still does not know what to do. What if her father does not come back? How long should she wait before she goes to look for him?

A few moments pass and she hears the sound of the front door closing again. Now she sees another figure cross the *yard*. Again, Sally's heart begins to *beat* faster. It is Mrs Larkin and she has Brutus by her side. They both cross the *yard* without making a sound and go down the side of the *barn*, where her father went only moments before.

Oh no, she thinks. What do I do now? She is feeling *frightened* and her heart is now *beating* like a *drum*.

Übung 10: Lesen Sie weiter und unterstreichen Sie die Substantive in Klammern im folgenden Abschnitt!
(1. Augen, 2. Scheune, 3. Tuch, 4. Fenster, 5. Boden, 6 Lieferwagen)

DI Rush opens his eyes and sees that he is inside the *barn*. He is sitting on a chair. When he tries to move, he finds that his hands are *tied* behind him and his feet are *tied* to the chair. Also, a piece of *cloth* has been pushed into his mouth. His head *hurts* and for a few moments he is not sure what happened. The last thing he *remembers* is looking through the window into the *barn*. He looks around him. He sees again the group of men, all of them black, that he saw through the window. They look like Africans. The men are sitting around on the floor of the *barn*. Most of them look tired and *frightened*. Each of them has a rucksack.
At that moment, Mr Larkin *appears* from behind the *van*. He looks across at DI Rush.

"Ah, Mr Rush. I see that you're awake," he says. "I knew that you would be a problem from the moment you arrived. Always asking questions, always looking where you shouldn't be looking. And you see what's happened. Now, I'll have to kill you."
DI Rush tries to answer, but he cannot speak because of the *cloth* in his mouth. Larkin comes across to him and pulls it out. The Africans watch in *silence*.
DI Rush *breathes* deeply before he speaks. "You don't have to kill me, I won't say anything. I know that you're bringing illegal *immigrants* into the country, but that isn't as *serious* as *murder*. Don't be stupid. If I *disappear*, my daughter will go to the police."
"Your daughter won't be able to go to the police," says Larkin in a very unfriendly tone of voice. "She will be dead as well."

"No!" *pleads* DI Rush. "Not Sally!"

"Yes," replies Larkin. "My wife has just gone to *fetch* her from her room." He begins to smile. "She's a very attractive girl, your daughter. If Mrs Larkin wasn't here, I could have some fun with her."

"You animal," *growls* DI Rush and *struggles* in the chair, but he cannot break the *wire* which is around his *wrists* and *ankles*. "You won't *get away with* this."

Larkin *grabs* the inspector's head and pushes the *cloth* back in his mouth.

"Oh, I think we will, Mr Rush," he replies. "This is our last job. We have been doing this for three years now. It seems that everyone wants to come to England. Most nights of the week a group of *immigrants* come across by boat from France. We meet them on the beach and bring them here. We give them a drink and a sandwich and then take them to London in the *van*. We get one thousand pounds for each one. Do you know how much money we have now, Mr Rush?"

DI Rush just stares silently at him, *hate* in his eyes. He knows that he cannot do anything to stop Larkin. Oh God, he thinks, I can't even warn Sally!

"Well, we have enough to start a new life in another country. Somewhere warmer than England. I don't want to work again, ever. I want to spend my time with beautiful girls." He laughs. "Don't tell Mrs Larkin, will you."

As he begins to walk away, he *adds*, "Well, I can't stand here talking all night. There's work to be done."

Suddenly they hear the sound of Brutus barking in the house.

"Perhaps your daughter is putting up a *struggle*," laughs Larkin. "I hope Brutus doesn't get hold of her. We don't want blood all over the house."

He walks to the *barn* door, opens it *slightly* and looks out. Then he returns and speaks to the Africans. “In,” he says and *points* to the back of the *van*. “London.”

The men pick up their rucksacks and begin to move towards the *van*. Some of them look at the inspector *tied* to the chair, but none of them do anything to help him. Silently, one by one, they climb into the back of the *van*. When they are all in, Larkin closes the doors.

He looks across at the DI. “We don’t want too many *witnesses*, do we, Mr Rush?” he says. “Not that we are going to kill you here. We’ll put you and your daughter in the *boot* of your car and drive it to London before we shoot you. By the time the police find you and discover who you are, we’ll be out of the country. As soon as Brenda gets back with your daughter, we can go.”

DI Rush tries to free himself, but the *wire* is *tied* too tightly. I will have to wait for the right moment, he thinks. Hopefully, I’ll have an *opportunity* to escape when they try to put me in the car.

For the moment, however, he can only sit, watch and wait.

Übung 11: Wie heißt das Verb im Simple Past?

1. begin ______________
2. tie ______________
3. shoot ______________
4. look ______________
5. say ______________
6. do ______________
7. come ______________
8. push ______________
9. see ______________
10. have ______________
11. put ______________
12. know ______________

Sally also sits, watches and waits. It is now several minutes since she saw Mrs Larkin and the dog *disappear* behind the *barn*. She has heard no sound and there has been no *movement* in the *yard*. She cannot decide what she should do. Should she continue to sit and wait? How long should she wait? What if her father does not come back? While she is thinking, the door of the *barn* opens. In the light from inside, Sally sees Mrs Larkin come out of the *barn* and close the door behind her. Brutus is by her side.

Perhaps everything is all right, thinks Sally. Dad must have heard her coming. He's probably still behind the *barn*.

She watches Mrs Larkin walk slowly across the *cobbled yard* and enter the house. For a few moments there is *silence* and then Sally hears a sound on the stairs. She goes to her bedroom door and listens. She can hear the sound of Brutus *growling* quietly.

What if they have done something to Dad and now they are looking for me, she thinks. In a second, they will come in here. She reaches for the key, but before she can turn it, the door begins to open. In the darkness, she sees a hand holding a pistol *appear* around the *edge* of the door. *Immediately*, Sally throws herself against the door, closing it hard on the arm holding the *gun*. There is a *scream* from outside and the pistol *clatters* to the floor. Brutus begins to bark loudly.

Sally is now able to close the door, and she pulls the chair over to hold it closed for as long as possible. She picks up the pistol and puts it into the *belt* of her jeans. She doesn't like to have it with her, but she can't leave it there for Mrs Larkin.

Now she has to escape. She knows that she could never shoot Mrs Larkin or Brutus – not even to *protect* her own life. I could probably *overpower* Mrs Larkin, she thinks, but I certainly can't fight the dog. All this flies through her mind *in an instant*. She runs to the open window and climbs out as Mrs Larkin begins to hit the door with something heavy. The window to her room and the window to her father's room are side by side.

"*Thank goodness*," she *gasps* as she sees that his window is open. From her window she is able to climb across to his and into his room. As she stands in his room, she hears the sound of the chair break and the door to her room opens with a crash.

"Kill, Brutus, kill!" *screams* Mrs Larkin and in a moment, Sally can hear Brutus barking in her room. Quickly, she picks up the heavy lamp from the bedside table and slowly opens the bedroom door. Mrs Larkin is standing outside Sally's bedroom door and is holding her *injured wrist*. She is waiting to hear Sally *scream* when Brutus has his teeth in her.

Silently, Sally steps behind her and, with all her strength, hits her on the back of the head with the lamp. Without a sound, Mrs Larkin falls to the floor *unconscious*. Sally steps over her body and quickly closes the bedroom door. Brutus is now a *prisoner* in the room. Sally *breathes* deeply and now that the danger is past, she begins to *tremble*.

"I don't know what it is that they're doing here," she says to herself, "but if Mrs Larkin came looking for me with a *gun*, it must be something illegal."

Now she thinks about her father. What can have happened to him? She will have to go to the *barn* and see if she can find him. First, however, she must do something with Mrs Larkin. Sally quickly *checks* to see if the woman is still *breathing*. Luckily, she is. The *blow* wasn't hard enough to kill her. Sally *grabs* her by the shoulders and *drags* her into her father's room. She uses the cable from the table lamp to *tie* Mrs Larkin's hands together. She then uses one of her father's *belts* to *fasten* the woman's legs together. Finally, she uses another *belt*. She puts it through Mrs Larkin's arms and *fastens* it around the leg of the bed.

ÜBUNG 12

Übung 12: Lesen Sie weiter und unterstreichen Sie die richtige Variante!

When she is happy that Mrs Larkin (1.) can/cannot escape, she takes the pistol from her *belt* and looks (2.) on/at it. The smooth, cold metal in her hand makes (3.) her/him feel *uncomfortable*. She places it back (4.) in/on her *belt* and *carefully* goes down the stairs. She stops at the bottom of the stairs and listens. Brutus has now stopped (5.) baking/barking. The house is in darkness and completely silent. Sally goes to the front door and (6.) closes/opens it slowly. The *yard* is dark and there is (7.) no/none sound. Where is Mr Larkin? (8.) Will/Should he come to the house to look for his wife? Hopefully, he is still in the *barn*.

Sally leaves the house and closes the door behind her. Quickly, she moves around the *edge* of the *yard* until she is at the side of the *barn*. She stands at the window where her father stood a short time ago and looks into the *barn*. She *gasps* as she sees her father *tied* to a chair. Mr Larkin is just closing the doors at the back of the *van* and is speaking to her father. She can't hear what he is saying, but from the look on her father's face, it is not something *pleasant*.
Larkin opens the two large *barn* doors before he climbs into the driver's seat of the *van*. As Sally watches, the *van* moves forward out of the *barn* and into the *yard*. Now is my *opportunity*, thinks Sally. She takes the pistol from her *belt* and then she opens the side door of the *barn*. After quickly looking around, she runs across to her father with the pistol in her hand. She places the pistol on the floor and throws her arms around him.
"Oh, Dad," she *gasps*. "Are you okay?"
All her father can do is *mumble*. He still has the *cloth* in his mouth, so she pulls it out.

"Behind you," he *gasps*.

Sally turns, but it's already too late. Larkin has silently come back into the *barn* and before she can move, he picks up the pistol from the floor. He steps back away from her and *points* the pistol at her heart.

"Well, well, Miss Rush," he says. "What a *pleasant surprise*. So nice of you to join us."

Chapter 4: Larkin Shoots

Sally and her father look at Larkin in *silence*.

"Where's my wife?" asks Larkin.

"In my Dad's bedroom," Sally replies. "She's *unconscious*, but *apart from* that she's okay. Oh, and I've *tied* her up."

"And Brutus?" asks Larkin. "I hope you haven't *injured* Brutus."

"No, of course not," says Sally. "He's locked in my bedroom."

"You're not just an attractive woman, are you?" continues Larkin. "I really have *underestimated* you. Unfortunately for you, I now have the pistol and I won't make the same mistake twice."

"What are you going to do with us?" asks Sally.

"He's going to kill us," answers DI Rush. "The *van* is full of illegal *immigrants* from Africa. He brings them into the country every week."

"Surely it's not worth killing us to *protect* your illegal little business, is it?" says Sally. "In a few days every policeman in England will be looking for you."

"When they find your bodies, we will be far away," replies Larkin. "Anyway, you aren't the first to die. What do you think happened to Mr Dalton?"

"So the blood in the *yard* was his?" *gasps* Sally.

ÜBUNG 13 !

Übung 13: Übersetzen Sie die Begriffe, um das Rätsel zu lösen!

1. überrascht _ _ _ _ _ ☐ _ _ _
2. klagen _ _ ☐ _ _ _ _ _
3. Trommel _ _ _ ☐
4. verletzen ☐ _ _ _ _ _
5. schmuddelig ☐ _ _ _ _ _
6. Scheune _ _ ☐ _
7. auspacken _ _ _ ☐ _ _
8. schließlich _ _ _ ☐ _ _ _ _ _ _
9. Pferdeschwanz _ _ _ _ ☐ _ _ _

Lösung: _ _ _ _ _ _ _ _ _

"Yes," answers Larkin. "I put him in the *boot* of his car before I drove it to London, so he was on the ground in the *yard* for a few minutes. That's where the blood came from. I didn't see it in the dark."

"But why did you kill him?" asks DI Rush.

"I can't stand around here all night talking," *growls* Larkin. "There's work to be done. That's your last question, Mr Rush. Dalton was our partner. He looked after the *immigrants* when they arrived in London. He found jobs and rooms for them. Then they had to pay him all the money that they *earned*. He was richer than we were. A few days ago, Brenda and I decided that we wanted to stop bringing in the *immigrants*. We're quite rich now and want to enjoy our money. Dalton wanted us to continue, but we said that we were leaving. He came here to try to *convince* us to stay. He even brought a pistol to help '*convince*' us."

Larkin laughs and *waves* the pistol around. "This pistol, in fact. When he *threatened* me with it, we *struggled* and I took it from him.

Then I shot him. I knew he would always be a danger for us if I left him alive."

He pauses a moment and then *adds*, "So you see, I'm already a *murderer*. I have no *choice*. I have to kill you both."

"You won't *get away with* it," cries DI Rush.

"I think I will. Now, Miss Rush, please lie on the floor and put your arms behind your back. I need to *tie* your hands together."

Without taking his eyes from Sally, he goes to the wall of the *barn* and gets some *wire*. He returns to stand in front of her, the *wire* in one hand and the pistol in the other.

Sally laughs. "Do you think I'm going to make it easy for you? There are several things you don't know about me, Mr Larkin. Firstly, I don't like someone telling me what to do. I am very *stubborn*. If you don't *believe* me, ask my Dad."

Übung 14: Lesen Sie weiter und bilden Sie sinnvolle Wörter aus dem Buchstabensalat!

The inspector sits there with his (1. thumo) ______________ open.

He cannot *believe* how *calm* his (2. readthug) ______________ is.

She is going to die and she is talking to Larkin as though they are

(3. guissscind) ____________________ the weather.

Larkin *points* the pistol at the (4. spinctore) ____________________.

"Either you do as I say, or your father gets the first *bullet*," he says.

"That's the second thing you don't know about me," (5. swearsn)

________________ Sally. "I hate (6. snug) ____________. I would like

to see them all *destroyed*."

"Just be quiet and lie on the floor," replies Larkin *impatiently*.

"Please let me finish," continues Sally. "As I said, I hate *guns*, so although I brought your wife's pistol with me, I took out all the *bullets* so that no one could use it."

As she finishes speaking, she begins to walk towards Larkin. He *points* the pistol directly at her and pulls the trigger. The only sound is a metallic "click". A look of anger *appears* on his face. He pulls the trigger a second time, only to hear the "click" again.

By now Sally is directly in front of him. As he *swings* the pistol at her head, Sally moves quickly to the side and *slides* her hand down his arm. This pulls him *off balance*. She then begins to turn and as she does, she takes hold of his *wrist* with one hand and *grabs* his head with the other. She pulls it against her shoulder and continues to turn. Larkin *swears*. He cannot *believe* this is happening. He really has *underestimated* her. She pushes his head towards the floor and he tries to stand up. Suddenly she is pushing him in the same direction. He is *upright* for only a second before he falls backwards, Sally's arm and body pushing him down. He hits the floor and the air is knocked out of his body. Sally still holds his *wrist* and now she uses his arm to turn him over, so that he is facing the floor. She picks up the *wire* that has fallen from his hand during the *struggle* and quickly uses it to *tie* his hands together. Then she stands up and *breathes* deeply.

"Are you okay, Sally?" asks the inspector.

"I'm fine, Dad," she replies. "Are you all right?"

"*Apart from* a bit of a headache, I've never felt better," he replies. "I always knew that I had an *amazing* daughter," he continues, "but until tonight, I never knew how *amazing* you really are. I'm so happy now that I paid for your Aikido courses."

"And I'm so happy that I took the *bullets* out of the pistol," replies Sally and smiles at her father.

Übung 15: Bilden Sie aus dem Adjektiv ein Substantiv!

1. lucky luck
2. happy ____________
3. silent ____________
4. dangerous ____________
5. surprised ____________
6. angry ____________
7. dark ____________

Three days later, Sally and her father are sitting on the grass at Leeds Castle. They have just eaten a picnic of sandwiches and wine, and they both feel relaxed and happy. It is a beautiful summer evening, and thousands of other people are sitting around them. They are all waiting for the start of the concert.

"There was a time when I thought we wouldn't be sitting here together tonight," says DI Rush, as he puts his arm around his daughter and *hugs* her.

"Yes," agrees Sally. "When Mrs Larkin came for me with the pistol and the dog, I didn't know what to do. It is a good thing that she didn't send Brutus in first. I think everything would have ended differently. Anyway, now that they are in *prison*, we can relax. I *suppose* that we'll have to come back to Kent when they *appear* in *court*?"

"Yes," answers her father. "That won't be for several weeks yet, though. The police have a lot of work to do before that. They told me that they have found Dalton's body in his car in London. Just as Larkin said. The pistol will have to be *checked* to see if it fired the *bullet* that killed him. They will also have to speak to all the Africans who were in the *van*."

"I really feel sorry for them," says Sally. "*Presumably* they will all be sent back to the countries that they came from?"

"I think so," replies the inspector. "But perhaps some of them will be able to stay."

"We are so lucky to live in this country, aren't we? And I'm *especially* lucky. I have such a good life here," says Sally as she *hugs* her father. "And I have people who love me."

"Indeed you do, Sally," says her father and smiles. "Indeed you do."

STOLEN SUMMER

Alison Romer

Chapter 1: Scary Stories

Michael Rose had been working for the Lancashire Police for seven years. He loved his job. Because he lived and worked in a small village, he knew many people by name. Even though he was only thirty-three, he was an *old-fashioned* type of policeman: friendly, caring and ready to help. He liked the people of Pendle Lee, and the people of Pendle Lee liked Sergeant Rose.

Crime was not a big problem. At the police station, days went by quite slowly. Many other officers liked to be in a bigger town or a city. But Michael loved being part of a small *community*. The village itself was also a lovely place to live. The church, which was in the centre, had been built in 1376. Many of the houses had been standing for a very long time. Even the pub, which was called "The White *Witch*", was hundreds of years old. At the *edge* of the village a river *flowed* through the fields and woods. On summer evenings it was as beautiful as a painting.

However, there was not very much for young people to do. Bored teenagers were often getting into trouble. In fact, most of the problems Michael had to *deal with* were caused by teenagers. Loud music, graffiti and bad *behaviour* were the main things. Usually he just talked to the young people and their parents. He hardly ever had to take one of them to the station. In seven years he had only *arrested* five people. Yet in those seven years he had found eleven lost dogs, and returned them to their homes. Some policemen would have found that kind of life boring. But Michael was happy.

ÜBUNG 1 !

Übung 1: Übersetzen Sie!

1. fields ______________________
2. village ______________________
3. caring ______________________
4. ancient ______________________
5. cottage ______________________
6. edge ______________________
7. happen ______________________
8. evening ______________________
9. gate ______________________
10. painting ______________________

It was the middle of summer. The sun had just *set* and it was very late. Michael was at the police station. He was on the night *shift*. For a few hours he had been doing some paperwork. Even in a small village station there was a lot of *bureaucracy*. He had also had some coffee and had read the newspaper. The police station cat, Harriet, was sitting on his knee. She was *purring*.

"Sorry, Harriet," Michael said. "You're going to have to move. I want another coffee." He tried to push the fat *tabby* cat off his lap, but she didn't want to go.

Suddenly the phone rang.

That's *strange*, Michael thought. Nobody ever called late at night unless something was really wrong.

He picked up the phone.

"Pendle Lee Police Station," he said.

"Oh, Michael," said a voice he *recognized*. It was Mrs White, an *elderly* lady who lived on the *edge* of the village.

"I'm sorry it's so late," she said. "But there's something happening in the *cemetery*."

Michael *sighed*. Every now and again a group of teenagers would gather at the Pendle Lee *Cemetery*. Wearing black clothes, they would light candles and play loud music.

"Is it those kids again?" Michael asked.

"Maybe," Mrs White replied. "I can't sleep. And it *upsets* me that they go to the *graveyard*. My parents' and grandparents' *graves* are there."

"Of course," said Michael. "I'll go *right away*. Then maybe you can get some sleep."

Übung 2: Welche ist die richtige Variante? Kreuzen Sie an!

ÜBUNG 2 !

1. The graveyard at night...
   a) ☐ looked how something from a scary movie.
   b) ☐ looked like something from a scary movie.
   c) ☐ looked as something from a scary movie.

2. Police work involves...
   a) ☐ much bureaucracies.
   b) ☐ more bureaucracy.
   c) ☐ a lot of bureaucracy.

3. He knew many people by name.
   a) ☐ He called people names.
   b) ☐ He knew lots of people quite well.
   c) ☐ Many people knew his name.

Around ten minutes later, Michael parked the police car at the *cemetery* gates. He could hear music. The yellow *glow* of candles told him where the kids were. He got out of the car and *switched on* his *torch*. Next to the gates was a very old house. In the past the *cemetery caretaker* had lived in it. But the place had been standing empty for twenty years. Some of the windows were broken. Climbing plants had grown over the building. They had even gone through some of the windows. Two hundred years ago it had been really pretty. But now it looked like something from a scary movie. Nobody went inside. Birds had made their homes in the empty rooms. Using his *torch* to light the way, Michael went towards the teenagers. Lots of candles were *glowing* on the *graves*. There was loud music, and some of the teenagers were standing in a circle singing.

When Michael *appeared* out of the darkness, he *frightened* some of them. A girl nearly *screamed*.

"Sorry," he said to her. "It's only me. Are you trying to make a *ghost appear*?"

"*It's none of your business,*" said a tall boy. He stepped forward into the torchlight. Michael knew who he was. His name was Alex. He was seventeen years old and his parents owned the bakery.

"It IS my business," Michael replied. "This is a *cemetery*. It's an important part of this *community*, and having a party here isn't respectful."

The girl who had nearly *screamed* came across to Michael.

"We can do what we want," she said. She was trying to sound *brave* after her *fright* earlier.

Michael *recognized* her now. Katie Lewis. She was only fourteen, and she should have been at home in bed.

"What are you doing?" Michael asked. "Are you trying to make contact with *witches*? I don't think you'll have any luck tonight."

Pendle Lee was in a part of Lancashire that was famous for its *witches*. In the early seventeenth century, some women and men from the area had been *arrested*. It was said that one talked to a black dog that was really the devil. The villagers *believed* that *witches* had made some people sick and even killed them. It was *believed* that cows stopped giving milk because of magic spells. The unlucky women and men were kept in *prison* at Lancaster Castle. The *witches* had been *hung* in 1612. Many people went to watch. Now the *witches* were seen as ordinary people who were *scapegoats* of the *community*. But the stories had continued until the present day. The Lancashire *Witches* brought many tourists to the area. People could buy toy *witches*. Lancaster Castle even had a special tour of the old *prison* rooms. And every year on Halloween, people from all over walked up Pendle Hill in the dark. Pendle Lee had its own stories, too. Some were about the *cemetery*. The first *graves* were over seven hundred years old. Long before the big Pendle Lee church was built, an even older church *existed* where the *cemetery* was. The stories told of *witches* meeting at the place where the old church once stood. It was said that they danced around large fires and tried to see the devil. The *ghost* of a *witch* called Agnes Cott was said to *haunt* the *graveyard*. Some people said that the *caretaker's* house was *haunted,* too. *Strange* noises were heard late at night. *Strange* lights were seen, too, even when the teenagers were in their beds.

Übung 3: Lesen Sie weiter und fügen Sie die passenden Wörter in die Lücken ein!
(nothing, stop, church hall, time, happier, noise)

Michael *switched on* his *torch* again.

"(1.) ______________ to go," he said to the kids, "before the *ghost* of Agnes Cott really does *appear*. Then you'll all run *screaming* back home anyway."

"You can't (2.) ______________ us," said Alex. "We'll come back again. The more this *community* hates us the (3.) ______________ we are."

"I'm sorry you feel that way," said Michael. He did understand. There was (4.) ______________ for teenagers to do in Pendle Lee. He thought that young people's discos at the (5.) ______________, were a good idea. The villagers were *worried* about (6.) ______________ and alcohol. However, having teenagers on the streets at night was a bigger problem.

After the kids left the *graveyard*, Michael looked around. There wasn't any graffiti on the *graves* tonight. In the past there had been a problem with graffiti. Even some of the *headstones* had been *smashed*. That was a few years ago. Alex and the other young people were angry and bored, but Michael didn't think they would do anything that bad. He decided to keep an eye on them anyway.

A few days later, Michael was on a normal afternoon *shift*. He liked to work during the day because there was more to do. He could walk around the village and talk to people. He could *stop by* the different shops and *chat* with the owners. At the station, other officers would come in from time to time. Even Harriet the cat liked the daytime best. On sunny days she could lie on the step outside the station. Anybody coming in or going out would have to step over her.

Mr Murphy, an *elderly* man, had called in at the station to give Michael some beans. Mr Murphy had grown them himself in his *allotment*. He was always *stopping by* with fresh vegetables. Like many older people, he used his *allotment* for pleasure rather than needing the food. He grew more than he could eat. Michael was just *admiring* the fresh green beans when his mobile rang.

"I'll just get that," Michael said to Mr Murphy.

He put the beans down. The call was from his boss, who had an office in the city.

"We've just heard from the Oswald Gallery," the Chief Inspector said. "They called the national *emergency* number. Can you go there, Michael? They've been *burgled*."

Michael *switched on* the *sirens* as he drove quickly through the village in his car. As he drove, he thought about the gallery. He hadn't been there for over three years, but he used to go a lot. That was because his ex-girlfriend, Sarah, loved art. Sarah had left to go to America about three years ago. She worked in *art restoration*, and had been *offered* a job in Boston. After *thinking long and hard*, she decided to take it. But Michael couldn't get a job with the police in the United States. He didn't want to stop being a policeman either. So he stayed in Pendle Lee and Sarah moved to Boston.

The Oswald Gallery was just outside the village. It was in a beautiful eighteenth-century house. A man called John Oswald had built the house, and the gallery was named after him. It took Michael around ten minutes to get there. When he arrived, he walked to the door. Two *elderly* women quickly came to meet him. They looked *upset*. Both of them started speaking *at once*.

"Oh Sergeant, *thank goodness* you're here!" one of the women *exclaimed*. "I'm Joan Potts. I work here."
"We don't know how it happened," the other lady was saying at the same time, "but it's my *fault*!"
"No, Lottie, of course it's not your *fault*," said Joan.
"Yes it is!" Lottie *exclaimed*. "I'm so angry with myself!"
Michael raised his hands.
"Let's stay *calm*," he said. "We'll go inside and you can tell me all about it. Then we'll start searching for the *thief*."

Chapter 2: Past Life

Once inside, Michael took out his notebook.
"Now tell me what happened," he said.
"No one had come to visit for over two hours," said Joan Potts. "It was a slow day."
Lottie Bingley sat down behind the *reception* desk.
"I'm afraid I left the *reception*," she said. "Every year we have a *competition* for artists. People from all over Lancashire send in their paintings. This morning we had some new paintings come in, and I was very excited. I wanted to see them, even though it's not my job to *unpack* them. I went upstairs to look. While I was gone, someone came in and *stole* one of our paintings. So it's all my *fault*."
Michael looked all around the room.
"Don't you have *security cameras*?" he asked.
"No," Joan replied. "It would cost a lot of money. But we never imagined that someone would *steal* from the Oswald Gallery!"
"And neither of you saw anybody?" Michael asked.
"No." Both women replied at the same time.

"We didn't see or hear anything," said Lottie.
"Let's have a look at where the painting was hung," Michael said.
The women led him into one of the gallery's little rooms. Modern galleries had lots of space and white paint, but the Oswald Gallery was different. The building had many small rooms and *halls*. The walls were covered in beautiful old wood. The windows were very small. As visitors walked around, they could imagine living three hundred years ago. Paintings were hung on all the walls, but in one place there was an empty spot.
"It was here," said Joan. "It was called 'Summer'."
Michael took out his phone.
"I'm going to call the *crime scene* police," he told Joan and Lottie. "Someone will come round and *check* for *fingerprints*. I'll also need a photograph of the painting, please. It'll help in the *investigation*."
"I'll go and find one," said Lottie. "The artist was Butterworth, of course."

The Oswald Gallery was small and not very important. But it had the largest collection of Butterworth paintings in the country. Tristan Butterworth was a famous painter from the 1940s and 50s. He had lived near Pendle Lee for many years. When he died in the 1980s, many of his best paintings were given to the gallery. People came from all over the United Kingdom to see them.

Übung 4: Setzen Sie die richtigen Fragepronomen ein!
(which, who, where, why, what, when)

ÜBUNG 4 !

1. ______________ was the painting hung?
2. ______________ kind of competition was it?

3. ______________ does the gallery open?

4. ______________ of the paintings was stolen?

5. ______________ were Joan and Lottie so upset?

6. ______________ works at the gallery?

Lottie came back into the *reception* and handed a large photograph to Michael.
"Here it is," she said. "'Summer'. It's a wonderful picture, isn't it?"
Michael looked at it. It showed a beautiful summer scene. In the *background* the sun shone on a river. Green fields and trees were all around. In the front of the painting there was a large tree, and under it sat a young woman. She was wearing an *old-fashioned* yellow dress and a big hat.
"This was painted in 1951," Lottie said. "Looking at it makes me feel so *calm*. It almost feels like you're really there."
"It's lovely," said Michael. "I'll need to keep this photograph for our *investigation*. Is that okay?"
"Of course," said Lottie. "We'll do whatever we can to help."

Back inside his car, Michael phoned his boss, Chief Inspector Blake. He gave Blake all the information he had so far. The inspector was very *busy*. Michael could tell he wasn't very interested in a painting *stolen* from a village gallery. The city had more crime than the police could *deal with*.
"They should have had *security cameras*," Blake said angrily.
He told Michael to contact the Art Loss Register. It kept an international database of art that had been *stolen* or lost. If a rich person or a museum wanted to buy a piece of art, they could find out if it was *stolen* through the Register. If it was, the buyer could *alert* the police. The *thief* who was trying to sell the art could then be caught.

It was hard to find *stolen* art. Sometimes the buyer knew it was *stolen*, but didn't care. Sometimes a group of *thieves* would plan a big *burglary*, and then wait for many years before selling the art in places like Africa or South America.

"Can you *deal with* this?" Blake asked Michael. "I don't have another officer who can come down there right now. It's too bad we have to send you a *crime scene* officer just to take some *finger-prints*."

"I still think it's a good idea," Michael said. The inspector was often in a bad *mood*, and Michael was glad he didn't have to work in the city with him.

"You know we're on 'terror *alert*', don't you?" Blake went on. "We may have to send officers to Manchester or London at any moment. You too, Sergeant."

"I know," Michael replied. "Leave everything to me, Inspector. I'll send you my reports."

After the phone call was finished, Michael opened the car window. He took a deep breath of fresh air. Then he looked at the photograph of 'Summer' again. The young woman in the picture was very pretty. She had long, *wavy* blonde hair. She looked out across the fields. Michael *wondered* if the woman had been real, or if she had come from the painter's *imagination*.

Michael was soon back at the station. He *immediately* contacted the Art Loss Register. He informed them about the *stolen* painting and gave all the *details*. Then he went out and *interviewed* the villagers. He was hoping someone had seen something *strange*, like someone hurrying away from the village. *Meanwhile* the *crime scene* officer was exploring the gallery. If *fingerprints* were found, they would be put into the police *fingerprint* database. If the *thief* had done anything wrong before, his (or her) prints would be in the database. They would match with the prints from the *crime scene*. Then the police would have a name.

Over the next two days Michael was *busy*. He put up signs about the *burglary*. The signs asked people with any information to call the police or the national *Crimestoppers number*. He also went from house to house, asking the villagers if they had seen a *stranger* in the village. A few couples and families had had picnics or had stopped at the White *Witch* pub. But nobody had been behaving *strangely*. He made copies of the 'Summer' photograph. Then he took them to all the art shops and *auction houses* in the area. He sent the photo to colleagues in Preston, Manchester, and even London.
At the station he put the photo on the wall. Instead of trying to find a *stolen* painting, he began to feel that he was trying to find the beautiful woman. It seemed very important to take her back to the gallery where she lived.

ÜBUNG 5 !

Übung 5: Lesen Sie weiter und finden Sie die zwölf regelmäßigen Verben!

After a few days, the other police officers started to joke about Michael's painting. He looked at it a hundred times a day. Sometimes, when he was talking to someone, his eyes would go to the photograph.
"Have you fallen in love?" some of the officers asked.
Michael no longer *chatted* with the villagers. He didn't seem to have time any more. Even Harriet the cat seemed in a bad *mood* because of 'Summer'. Michael only wanted to hunt for the painting, and was no longer interested in playing with her.

1. ________________________

2. ________________________

3. ________________________

4. ________________________

5. ________________________

6. ________________________

7. ________________________

8. ________________________

9. ________________________

10. ________________________

11. ________________________

12. ________________________

Whenever he had a moment, he was on the phone or visiting *auction houses*, asking about the painting. Even when he was not at work, he'd visit places that sold old paintings.

On Tuesday afternoon, the phone rang. It was exactly five days since 'Summer' had been *stolen*. Every time the phone rang, Michael hoped it was about the painting. It was Joan Potts from the gallery.

"Something terrible has happened!" she *exclaimed*. "Lottie has been taken to hospital. Another painting was *stolen*, and this time the *thief* pushed Lottie down the stairs. She's *unconscious*."

After going *straight* to the gallery and looking at the *crime scene*, Michael went to the hospital with Joan. They were both very *worried* about Lottie. Because she was old, her chances of getting better quickly were not good. She'd hit her head quite badly, and broken one of her legs.

Joan couldn't help crying as they stood in the waiting room at the hospital. The doctor in charge promised to call Michael as soon as there was a change. Michael needed to ask her about what happened. Perhaps Lottie saw the *thief* coming up the stairs. But while she was *unconscious* and in danger, all he could do was wait and hope.

Meanwhile, he needed to contact the Art Loss Register about the second *stolen* painting. It was another Butterworth, called 'Evening in June'. This time it was of a terrace outside a lovely old house. There was a table with teacups and a teapot, and a large strawberry cake. On one of the chairs sat a woman. Michael *recognized* her as the woman from 'Summer'. This time she was dressed in a pretty purple dress. She was reading a book. In the *background* were green hills and the sun was just going down. The sunset seemed to make the picture *glow*.

Michael thought it was *strange* that both paintings were of the same woman. There were many Butterworth pictures that showed *landscapes* or still-life scenes. Only a few had the young woman in them. Perhaps that was a *clue*.

"Who was she?" Michael asked when he called Joan that night.

"Don't you know?" asked Joan. "It's Sylvia. Sylvia and Tristan Butterworth got married in 1950. She was very beautiful and was his model for some of his paintings."

"Maybe if we find out more about Sylvia Butterworth, it might give us a *clue*," Michael said. "Perhaps the *thief* wants to collect paintings of her."

"Good idea," said Joan. "Maybe he's *obsessed* with her. We have an *archive* at the gallery. It has a lot of information about Sylvia in it. You can look at it if you like."

Übung 6: Finden Sie das passende Gegenteil!

1. ☐ few	a) strange
2. ☐ push	b) quiet
3. ☐ wrong	c) pull
4. ☐ friendly	d) ugly
5. ☐ normal	e) many
6. ☐ slow	f) right
7. ☐ daytime	g) fast
8. ☐ beautiful	h) unfriendly
9. ☐ loud	i) night-time

The next day, after his afternoon *shift*, Michael went back to the Oswald Gallery. It had been closed, and there were plans to buy *security cameras*. The risk of someone getting *hurt* again was too big. Joan took Michael upstairs to a small office. It was filled with *filing cabinets*.

"This is the Butterworth *archive*," Joan said. "The *filing cabinets* are full of photographs and letters. They belonged to both Tristan and Sylvia. There are also lots of papers about Butterworth's paintings and *exhibitions*. You can look through them, if you like."

Joan made him a cup of coffee. Then she gave him the keys to the gallery and the code number of the alarm system. She went back to the hospital, where she spent her evenings sitting with Lottie. Michael was left alone. He didn't know where to start looking. All he knew was that someone had a *reason* for *stealing* Butterworth's paintings of Sylvia. Perhaps the past would give him a *clue*.

First he pulled open some *files* of photographs. There were lots of black and white ones. There were many of Sylvia by herself. Michael knew they were not important for the *investigation*, but he couldn't help looking. Some were of Sylvia when she was very young. Most showed her in her twenties and thirties.

Michael felt that he had never seen anyone more beautiful. Sylvia had big, dark eyes and a *glowing* smile. She was quite tall and looked strong and *confident*. When she was younger, she had worn her long hair down. When she was older, she wore it up, in the style of the 1950s. Her clothes were always pretty and looked good on her. In some of the photos, she was with a man. Michael *recognized* him as Tristan Butterworth. The names, places and dates were written on the backs of many photos. There were many pictures, for example, of Tristan and Sylvia in a *gorgeous landscape*. In the *background* were lakes and mountains. On the backs of the pictures were the words '*Honeymoon*, Cumbria, 1950'. The couple looked very happy. Some of the photographs showed other people, too. There were many that had been taken on the terrace of a house. Michael thought it was the same terrace as in 'Evening in June'. In the photos lots of people were standing around. They had glasses of wine and cigarettes. In other photos the same people were sitting under a tree, having a picnic. Behind them the Pendle Lee river *flowed*. Everyone was smiling at the camera. There were a few pictures of Butterworth with another man. The pictures said 'Nigel and Tristan', with different places and dates. There were also pictures of 'Nigel and Sylvia'.

Next he looked at some old letters. There were lots from Sylvia to Tristan. Michael began to read. He read for a long time. When he looked at his watch, he had been reading for over an hour. He had been in a different world. It seemed as though Sylvia was writing to him. He put down the letters and picked up some different ones. All of them were to Sylvia from a man named Nigel Huxley. Some were dated from 1941 to 1944, and had been sent from France.

Michael looked through them quickly. Huxley had written about being a *soldier* in World War II. He wrote about being *frightened* when bombs fell close by. He also told her about other *soldiers* who had died. Some of the letters were very *serious*. But others were full of fun. In these light letters, he wrote about parties and friends. Huxley had written 'To my darling Sylvia' at the top of the letters. It was clear that he had been in love with her. Michael took out his notebook and wrote down Nigel's name. Perhaps he was still alive. Maybe he had more information about Sylvia and the paintings.

Übung 7: Lesen Sie weiter und tragen Sie die Vergangenheitsformen der angegebenen Verben ein!

Michael had been in the *archive* for hours. At last he (1. decide) ______________ to go home. He wanted to come back as soon as possible, because there (2. are) ______________ many more letters and papers to look at. But before he (3. leave) ______________, Michael opened the *filing cabinet* with the photos. There was one he wanted to see again. The photo (4. show) ______________ Sylvia sitting on a beach. She was wearing a big sun hat and a white dress. Her hair (5. is) ______________ down. In her hands was a small book. She had (6. stop) ______________ reading and was looking into the camera. But instead of smiling, Sylvia looked *serious*. Michael (7. feel) ______________ that she was looking right at him. Before he could stop himself, he had (8. pick) ______________ up the photo.

Then he put it into his pocket. He had never *stolen* anything in his life. Now he was a *thief*, just like the person who had taken the paintings.

Michael had spent many hours in the *archive*, and it was now night-time. On his way home, he drove past the *cemetery*. He was *worried* that the teenagers were there again. Suddenly, he saw something. It looked like the *glow* from a candle or a *torch*. It seemed to be moving *among* the *graves*.
"Those kids!" Michael said out loud.
He looked at his watch: 12:16 a.m.
Michael stopped the car at the gates and got out his *torch*. Then he went into the *cemetery*. The light seemed to have *disappeared*. He listened, but couldn't hear anything. The moon was shining brightly and the air smelled like cut grass and old flowers. He walked on. The *graves* looked quite scary in the dark. Although he didn't *believe* in *ghosts*, Michael didn't feel very *brave*. It was like a *graveyard* scene from a scary movie.
Suddenly he got angry. The teenagers were probably *hiding* from him. Maybe Alex and his friends were all sitting behind the *head-stones*, waiting for him to go away. They probably thought this was funny. Michael decided to *switch off* his *torch* and wait for the kids to come out.
The moonlight helped him to see quite well. But suddenly a cloud moved across the sky and the moonlight *disappeared*. It was very dark. Michael turned around in a circle. Nothing. No light. And he still couldn't hear anything, either.
He was about to *switch* his *torch* back *on* when he saw a small light. It was near the old *caretaker's* house. There was someone there. Michael put on his *torch* again. He shone it across the *graves* towards the empty old house.

Übung 8: Welches Wort passt nicht in die Reihe? Finden Sie das „schwarze Schaf"!

ÜBUNG 8 !

1. love, hate, look, fear
2. paint, cook, photograph, draw
3. moonlight, torchlight, sunlight, starlight
4. pretty, strange, weird, bizarre
5. calm, peaceful, interesting, quiet
6. ghost, witch, vampire, murderer
7. steal, rob, burgle, sell
8. box, circle, triangle, square
9. graveyard, museum, headstone, cemetery
10. torch, candle, soldier, lamp
11. caretaker, ghost, painter, policeman
12. clue, confident, obsessed, frightened

"Hello!" he called out.

Immediately the candlelight *disappeared*. Michael started to walk.

"It's Sergeant Rose here," he shouted. "What are you doing?"

When he reached the house, he shone his *torch* all around. There was nobody there. However, a *strange* symbol had *appeared* on the front door. It showed three stars inside a circle, painted in yellow paint. He tried the door, but it wouldn't open. He went up to some of the windows and shone his *torch* inside. The rooms were empty *apart from* some broken tables and chairs. There were spider's *webs* everywhere.

"Whoever you are," Michael said to the empty air, "you should go home."

Suddenly he heard a ghostly laugh. He couldn't tell if it was a man's or a woman's voice. Before he could turn around there was a *sharp* pain in his head, and he was falling towards the ground.

Chapter 3: Young Woman with Flowers

When Michael finally opened his eyes, his clothes were wet from lying in the grass for a long time. He put his hand to his head. When he looked at his hand, there was something dark on his fingers. Blood. He felt sick and his head *hurt*. His *torch* was lying on the ground, but it wasn't working any more. Michael looked around. He didn't know what to do. The best thing would be to call his boss, then go to the hospital and get a doctor to look at him. He stood up. All he wanted to do was get into bed. He slowly went back to his car and drove home.

Early the next morning, Michael went to the station. He wrote a report about what happened in the *graveyard*. His head still *hurt* badly, but he didn't want to spend the day waiting to see a doctor. Instead he called the hospital about Lottie. She was still *unconscious* and the doctors were doing all sorts of tests. After the hospital call, he phoned the homes of Alex and some of the other teenagers from the *cemetery*. He asked their parents to bring them down to the station as soon as possible. If Alex had hit Michael, he was in *serious* trouble. Then he arranged for another officer to talk to the teenagers. Although Michael wanted to talk to Alex and the others himself, he was a *witness* to a crime. He couldn't be the questioning officer, too. Then Michael searched the Internet for Nigel Huxley. Huxley might have information about the paintings or Sylvia. He found out that Huxley had also been an artist. He was a *sculptor*, but he was not as famous as Butterworth. His last *sculpture* was made in 1967. Now Huxley lived in a village only 20 kilometres from Pendle Lee. He was 85 years old, and it seemed that he was very rich.

Michael thought about everything he now knew about Huxley. He

lived *nearby* and knew about art. And although he was old, you didn't have to be fit to push an old lady downstairs. He had been in love with Sylvia. Perhaps he had driven to the gallery. He could have *stolen* 'Summer' while Lottie was looking at the new paintings upstairs. The second time, Lottie may have seen him *stealing* 'Evening in June'. He might have pushed her down the stairs, then put the painting in the car and driven home.
Michael decided to pay Huxley a visit. But first he put out some cat food for Harriet. The big *tabby* was still in a bad *mood*. Michael just wanted to talk about, think about and dream about those paintings! He had no time for cats or the other villagers. When Mr Murphy came in that morning with a bag of aubergines, Michael had simply thanked him and looked back at the computer.

Übung 9: Lesen Sie weiter und setzen Sie die passenden Synonyme ein!
(elderly, looked, lots of, nearby, happy, lovely, large)

ÜBUNG 9 !

At lunch time, Michael drove to the (1. close by) ______________ village. It took him a long time to find Huxley's house. The house was very (2. big) ______________. In fact, it was a *mansion*, but it was hidden behind (3. many) ______________ trees on the *edge* of the village. Michael parked the police car in front of the house. It was a (4. wonderful) ______________ old place. There were lots of steps leading to a big door. Michael went up and rang the bell. After a few moments, an (5. old) ______________ woman opened the door. "Mrs Huxley?" Michael asked.

"No, I'm the *housekeeper*," the woman said. She (6. stared) ____________ at his police uniform and car. For some *reason*, she didn't seem too (7. *pleased*) ____________.

"Do you want to see Mr Huxley?"
"Yes, please, if he's at home," Michael replied.
"You'd better come in," said the *housekeeper*.
Michael followed her into the house.
"Wait here." The *housekeeper pointed* to a chair by the door.
She wasn't friendly at all. Michael *wondered* if she ever smiled. He sat down. The big *hall* was painted a light green. The floor was made of *gorgeous* dark wood. In the corner stood a large *sculpture*. Michael couldn't really tell what it was. It could have been a woman with long *wavy* hair. Or a tree. Whatever it was, it looked very modern.
Suddenly the *housekeeper appeared* again.
"You can see Mr Huxley now," she said. "He's in the living room."

Nigel Huxley sat in a big chair. He didn't look 85 at all. He seemed a lot younger. But perhaps that was because of his bright blue eyes. He looked intelligent and full of energy.
"I'm sorry about my *housekeeper*," Huxley said. "She's not very nice to visitors, even policemen."
Michael looked around the living room. The sun was shining through the large windows. There were two huge sofas and a few chairs. In the middle of the room was a round table. Lots of books were everywhere: on the table, on bookshelves and on the floor. There was also a beautiful old *fireplace*. Above the *fireplace*, on the wall, there was a painting. Michael *immediately recognized* Sylvia.
"That's a Butterworth picture!" he *exclaimed*.

"Yes," Huxley said. "It's called 'Young Woman with Flowers'. Tristan Butterworth gave it to me."
The painting showed Sylvia holding lots of flowers. They were pink, orange and red. The *background* was a dark green, and Sylvia was wearing a green dress.
Michael couldn't take his eyes off the picture. Even when the *housekeeper* came in with tea and biscuits, he couldn't stop looking at Sylvia.
"How can I help you?" Huxley asked, taking a cup of tea and a chocolate biscuit.
Michael finally took his eyes off the painting and looked at the old man. "I'm sorry, Mr Huxley, I should have introduced myself. I'm Sergeant Rose from the police station at Pendle Lee. You heard about the robbery at the gallery?" asked Michael.
"Of course," Huxley replied. "I collect Butterworth paintings. I'm often at the Oswald Gallery."
"You know that Lottie Bingley is *unconscious* in hospital?" Michael asked, watching Huxley closely.
"Yes. It's very sad and *upsetting*," Huxley said.
Michael looked at the picture of Sylvia above the *fireplace*.
"Somebody wanted those pictures very badly," he said. "Badly enough to almost kill an *elderly* woman. Both paintings were of Sylvia. I think we should look for someone who is *obsessed* with her."
Huxley's eyes shone and he gave a small smile.
"So you've come to question me," he said. "Good detective work, Sergeant Rose. It's true, I was in love with Sylvia. She and I grew up together. Our families were friends. We lived in the same village and went to the same church. Even when I was a teenager, I loved her. I met Tristan Butterworth at art school. Sylvia would model for us both. Then the Second World War started. I became a

soldier, but Tristan couldn't join the army. He had polio when he was a baby and there was something wrong with his leg. While I was in France, Tristan and Sylvia fell in love. I wanted them to be happy, so we stayed friends."

"What happened to Tristan and Sylvia?" Michael asked. He'd almost forgotten about the *stolen* art.

"The Butterworths moved to America in the 1960s," Huxley went on. "We wrote letters at Christmas, but after a few years our letters stopped. I heard they were living in New York. Tristan had an *exhibition* at the Museum of Modern Art. Then I read in the paper that he had died in 1986. I never saw Sylvia again. I tried to find her, but with no luck. Now my paintings of Sylvia bring back wonderful *memories* of summer."

"Would you *break the law* to get more of those *memories*?" Michael asked.

"I'm sorry to *disappoint* you," said Huxley, "but I didn't *steal* those paintings."

"So you won't mind if I look around your house?" Michael asked.

"Yes, I do mind, Sergeant Rose," the old man replied, standing up. "My house is private. If you don't have a *search warrant*, please leave."

Huxley was starting to get angry. But Michael knew he was right. Without a *search warrant*, the police couldn't search someone's home. Michael had to leave. He thanked Huxley for his time.

On his way out to the car again, he thought about the old man. Firstly, he seemed *obsessed* with Sylvia and collected paintings of her. Secondly, he was familiar with the Oswald Gallery and lived close by. Thirdly, he didn't want the police looking around his house.

Michael decided to call Chief Inspector Blake to find out if he could get a *search warrant* for the *mansion*.

Übung 10: Lesen Sie weiter und unterstreichen Sie die richtige Variante!

Later that night, Michael (1.) decided/decide to go to the gallery. He wanted to look in the *archives* again, and still (2.) have/had the key. He wasn't really (3.) thought/thinking about the *investigation*. He was (4.) *wondering*/wandering if Sylvia was still alive in New York or somewhere else. She would be an old woman (5.) by/until now. In his *imagination*, however, she was a beautiful young woman. He (6.) was wanting/wanted her to stay that way. He still (7.) kept/keeped the photo of Sylvia in his *wallet*. Every now and then, he (8.) taked/took it out and looked at it. Before he (9.) left/leaving for the gallery, he called Joan Potts. He wanted to let her (10.) know/now that he would visit the archive.

Now that the gallery was closed, she *believed* the paintings would be safe. However, she was still happy to know that a policeman was around. She also told him that they had bought a new security system. There were cameras for every room. In two days' time it would be installed. Then they could open the gallery again. *Meanwhile*, Lottie was out of danger. She could open her eyes and talk a little bit. She had no *memories* at all of the robbery. She was *confused* about being in the hospital. Still, Michael was *relieved* that she was getting better.

Chapter 4: Voices in the Dark

By the time Michael got to the Oswald Gallery, the sun had nearly *disappeared*. He parked his car right in front of the door, and was *shocked* about what he saw. There was graffiti all over the front of the building. It was the same yellow paint that he'd seen at the *caretaker's* house, and the same symbols. Then he saw the broken window. The hole was big enough for someone to climb through, but bits of glass were still *sharp*. The robber had probably been *hurt*. Michael looked through the broken window. A big rock from the garden was lying inside, on the wooden floor. Bits of broken glass were everywhere. On one piece of glass he saw something red. It looked like blood. The *thief* had been cut. This meant that the police could get an important DNA *clue*. Michael *immediately* took out his mobile phone. He called the city station. Another officer would come to Pendle Lee as soon as possible. The *crime scene* officer would come, too.

Michael didn't want to stand outside waiting. He decided to go in. Perhaps the *thief* was still in the gallery. Trying to stay *calm*, he opened the front door. Then he stopped and listened. He couldn't hear anything. He took another step. The wooden floor made a loud noise. Then, slowly and quietly, he went to the room with the broken window. There were paintings on the wall. Some of them were *landscapes* from the Butterworth collection. There were also *sculptures*. But Michael was more interested in the blood. It was a very dark red because it was almost dry. It made a small *trail* across the floor and into the *hall*. Michael followed it. The *trail* went up the stairs, along the *hall*, and into another room. It stopped in front of a wall. There was an empty space where a painting once hung.

! ÜBUNG 11

Übung 11: Ersetzen Sie die in Klammern stehenden Personen durch die richtigen Pronomen!

1. (Lottie) *She* was pushed down the stairs.
2. (Two policemen) ________ were helping with the investigation.

3. (You and I) __________ don't know who the thief is.

4. (Michael) __________ followed the trail of blood upstairs.

5. Michael told (Lottie and Joan) __________ to get cameras.

6. Can you tell (my friend and I) __________ where the gallery is?

7. We will visit (Lottie) __________ in the hospital.

8. Tell (Michael) __________ about the stolen painting!

Suddenly, there was a shout from downstairs. The two other policemen had arrived. Michael went downstairs and greeted them. He told them about the *trail* of blood and the *stolen* painting.
"Can you go through the rest of the building?" he asked the constable, whose name was John Ritchie. "I'm going to look in the garden."
"I'll get *fingerprints* and blood," said the *crime scene* officer. "But I don't think we'll get a match. There were no matches on our *fingerprint* database last time."
Just as Michael was about to go outside, the constable called him back.
"You're the one who was hit in the *graveyard*, aren't you?" he asked. "I talked to those teenagers. Every single one has an alibi. Even Alex, who is an angry young man. One day he'll end up *arrested* for something, *believe* me!"
Michael thanked him, then took his *torch* and went outside. There was no moonlight, so it was very dark. He walked all around the building, looking and listening. On one side of the garden was the car park. Two police cars were parked there. On the other side of the garden there were woods. They made a good *hiding* place. Michael went into the trees. It was very dark, almost black. The

trees looked very tall in the white light from the *torch*. Michael thought about his visits to the *cemetery*. Now he was walking through woods at night. His *torch* had become his best friend. It was a good thing he did not *believe* in *ghosts* or *witches*. If they were real, he would have seen one by now. In fact, he felt like the *ghost* of Pendle Lee himself. That's what happened when you spent too much time in *graveyards* and dark places.

Suddenly, he heard a noise. He *immediately* stopped walking and listened. He *wondered* if it was a small animal making noises in the dark. But then he heard a voice. Another voice answered. Two people were *hiding* in the woods. Michael took out his phone and called PC Ritchie. He spoke very quietly and quickly. The constable agreed to join him.

In less than a minute the constable was there, walking softly through the trees. Then they both *switched off* their *torches*. After a few moments, their eyes could see better in the darkness. They quietly walked towards the sound of voices. Two people were *hiding* in some bushes underneath a tree. They were dressed all in black, and had long black hair. This just made their white faces stand out even more in the dark. Michael *recognized* two young men from the *cemetery*. He gave a shout. The boys looked around and saw the officers, then jumped up and started to run. Michael and PC Ritchie raced after them through the trees. The teenagers were fast, but *frightened*. They kept looking behind them. Suddenly one of them hit a tree and fell to the ground.

"It's a good idea to look where you're going," said Michael as he pulled the boy to his feet. *Meanwhile*, PC Ritchie had managed to stop the other one. The constable took the boy's rucksack and opened it. He shone his *torch* inside.

"What do we have here, boys?" PC Ritchie asked, shining his light on cans of yellow *spray paint*.

At the police station, Michael and PC Ritchie questioned the teenagers. They said they'd painted the symbols on the walls, but had had nothing to do with the *smashed* window or the *burglary*. Just after doing the graffiti, they'd heard someone walking through the car park. They'd gone into the woods, and then heard the sound of breaking glass. One of the boys' fathers was in the room with them, which was normal when a 15-year-old was *involved* in a crime.

"Why didn't you call the police?" he asked his son.

"I hate the pigs," said the boy, using the *insulting* word for policemen. "Can we go now?"

Übung 12: Lesen Sie weiter und fügen Sie die Übersetzung der deutschen Wörter ein!

! ÜBUNG 12

The police would wait until daylight to (1. suchen) ________________ the woods for the *stolen* painting. Michael didn't want to let the boys go until then, but he had to. There was no (2. Grund) ________________ for *arresting* them. They were (3. geprüft) ________________ for cuts, because of the broken glass in the gallery window. But (4. keiner von beiden) ________________ the boys had been cut (5. irgendwo) ________________ on their bodies. They were in lots of trouble about the graffiti, but Michael didn't think (6. irgendetwas) ________________ *serious* would happen to them. He let them go home with their (7. Eltern) ________________.

Back at his desk, he made some notes for his report. Then he made a list of things to do in the morning. At the top was the *search warrant* for Nigel Huxley's home. He wanted to visit the old *sculptor* as soon as possible. He wanted to have some of Huxley's blood for testing, too. The investigators could match it against the blood from the gallery. Next, he wanted to take Joan Potts to the gallery to ask her about the *stolen* painting. He was sure it was another one of Sylvia. Then, he wanted to go to the hospital to see if Lottie had any *memories* of the robbery. Suddenly, the phone rang. Michael picked it up.

"Hello?" he said.

"Michael, it's Mrs White," said the woman on the phone. "Sorry I'm calling so late. It's those kids in the *cemetery*."

"Not again." Michael *sighed*. He was *disappointed*. There were bigger things than bad *behaviour* going on in Pendle Lee.

"I'll go *immediately*," he said. It wasn't illegal to be at a *cemetery* at night, but it wasn't respectful.

"Perhaps we can ask the *ghost* of Agnes Cott to give them a *fright*," Mrs White said. "Then they'll stay at home every night!"

Michael gave a short laugh.

"I'll ask her to pay them a visit," he said.

Once more, Michael drove to the *cemetery*. Once more, he parked at the gates and got out his *torch*. There were candles *glowing among* the *graves*. He could see young people sitting around. Loud music was playing. He *recognized* the tall figure of Alex. When he got close to the group, Alex saw him and stood up. The young man looked angry. Michael felt angry, too, but he didn't want to get *involved* in a fight with teenagers.

"Go away!" Alex *yelled*. Michael was just about to reply when he heard a loud *scream*. It sounded like it was coming from the *care-*

taker's cottage. *Immediately* Michael started to run to the old house. Alex ran, too.

"It's Katie!" Alex *exclaimed*. "She went into the house for a *dare*."

"Can't you kids stay out of trouble?" Michael shouted as he ran. When he got to the house, he tried to open the door. It was still locked shut.

"She went through a window," said Alex.

Together they ran to the side of the building. Just then Katie *screamed* again. Michael found the window. It was *old-fashioned*, and the old wood had made it easy to open from the outside. He shone his *torch* inside and called Katie's name. He saw her *rush* into the room, looking very *frightened*. When she saw Michael and Alex she started to cry and *immediately* tried to climb through the window. Michael helped her.

Once outside, Katie fell on the ground. She lay on the grass.

"It's the *witch*!" she said. She couldn't stop crying.

"What did she look like?" Alex asked.

Michael looked at the young man angrily. "There are no *witches*," he said. "Or *ghosts*." Then he saw a *strange glow* coming from inside the house. It was very bright orange.

Katie and Alex saw it, too.

"I dropped my candle," said Katie.

The old house was *on fire*.

Michael *immediately* pulled his mobile phone from his pocket. He called the *emergency* number. But just as he was about to speak, he saw a figure inside the house.

"There's someone in there!" he *exclaimed*.

"The *witch*!" Katie cried. "I told you. She's real!"

Michael threw the mobile to Alex, who *immediately* told the *emergency* services where they were. Then Michael climbed through the broken window into the *burning* house.

"Police!" he called out, but the figure had *disappeared*. He ran through the room and into the *hall*. Spider's *webs* were on his face and in his hair. The fire seemed to come from the front room. He could feel how hot it was. He was *choking* on heavy *smoke*. He looked around, *confused*. Then he saw her: a woman was going up the stairs. He had no time. The fire was going to *burn* the old building down. He ran up the stairs. He could see quite well because of the orange *glow* from the fire. When he got to the top, he saw her standing very still, looking at him. For a moment, he thought that Katie was right. The woman was a *witch*.

Agnes Cott, he thought. She had long grey hair and dirty old clothes. She looked very old. Michael told her his name.

"I'm here to help you," he said.

She turned and ran down the corridor. Michael followed her.

He could see *smoke* from the fire coming up the stairs. He went into one of the bedrooms. Although it was darker in the room, he could see the old woman. She was trying to pick up some large, flat objects. When Michael got closer, he saw that the objects were paintings. On every one, he *recognized* Sylvia. The old woman looked at Michael and started to cry.

"Please help me!" she said.

! ÜBUNG 13

Übung 13: Geben Sie die Pluralform an!

1. thief ______________________
2. woman ______________________
3. gallery ______________________
4. information ______________________

5. memory ______________________

6. noise ______________________

7. system ______________________

8. witch ______________________

9. torch ______________________

10. robbery ______________________

Two months later, after his evening *shift*, Michael left the station. He walked up the road. When he got to the *old people's home*, he stopped. Nigel Huxley was waiting for him. It was the same every Wednesday and Sunday. The two men went inside together.

Sometimes Sylvia couldn't *remember* their names. She couldn't *remember* pushing Lottie down the stairs, or laughing and knocking Michael out in the *graveyard*. For weeks she'd been living in the old *caretaker's* cottage. She *stole* things to eat, as well as the paintings. She couldn't be put in *prison* for her crimes because she had Alzheimer's disease. Instead, at the *old people's home* she had food, clothing and good care. She mainly *remembered* things that happened sixty years ago. Michael knew she had been beautiful then, although he couldn't tell from looking at the old woman now. He and Nigel would listen to her stories about wonderful summer evenings, and her eyes would *glow* with happiness.

"Her eyes are the one thing that hasn't changed," Michael said to Nigel, looking at the photo of Sylvia in his *wallet*. "They're still beautiful."

DEATH WISH

Andrew Ridley

Chapter 1: Death on a Damp Morning

Susan Hanson stands and looks out of the house window. The rain is falling on the garden. The leaves of the trees that stand along the side of the road are wet and very green. I am so lucky to live here, Susan thinks. Bramhope is so much better than the centre of Leeds. She thinks about when she was a child and the old house in a dirty street where she lived. Now she has a house with five bedrooms in one of the best areas of Leeds. But money and big houses are not really important when you are not happy. Why have five bedrooms when you do not have any children? Also, the letters which her husband *receives* make her unhappy. When she sees the postman come up to the door, Susan begins to *worry*. It is the same every day. Since the first letter came, she does not like seeing the postman.

She goes to the door and picks up the *pile* of letters from the floor and looks through them. Her hand begins to *shake* as she sees the writing on one of the envelopes. It is *strange* writing, thin and not in *straight* lines. It looks as though someone who is right-handed has written with their left hand. It is addressed, as usual, to her husband.

"Phillip," she calls, her voice full of emotion. "Phillip, there's another one of those letters." He *swears* in the kitchen and she hears the noise as he pushes his chair back and his footsteps come down the corridor. He meets her in the *hall*, an angry look on his face. He holds out his hand and she gives the envelope to him. He looks down at the writing.

"There's no *doubt* about it. It's the same writing as on the other two," he says angrily. He goes back to the kitchen. Susan follows him quietly. She watches as he takes a knife from the *drawer* and cuts open the envelope. He pulls out the single sheet of white paper. He holds it *carefully* by one corner. Susan knows that the police have asked him to *handle* any further letters with care. They do not want to lose any *forensic evidence*.

Übung 1: Trifft die Aussage zu?
Markieren Sie mit richtig ✔ oder falsch – !

ÜBUNG 1 !

1. When Susan looks out, the sun is shining. ☐
2. When she was young, she lived in an old house. ☐
3. She thinks that money is more important than anything else. ☐
4. When Susan sees the postman, she is happy. ☐
5. Her husband uses a knife to open the envelope. ☐
6. He holds the letter carefully because it is expensive. ☐
7. Their house has five bedrooms. ☐
8. The address has been written by hand. ☐

She watches as he places the letter on the table. He uses the knife to open it out. She can *immediately* see that the message has been made in the same way as the others. Someone has cut letters out of a newspaper and has *stuck* them to the paper. She *gasps* as she reads the *chilling* message on the paper.
Phillip reads the three words aloud. "You will die." He stops and then after a few seconds he *adds*, "Whoever sent this will be the one to die, if I get my hands on him."
"Oh, Phillip," says Susan. "I'm so *frightened*. Who can it be? Who could hate you so much? Why would anyone want to send these

horrible messages? It must be someone who is ill, sick in the head."

Since the first letter came, she has spent many hours thinking about it. Who could have sent it? Phillip has worked as a builder since he left school. During the past twenty years his business has grown. Now, thirty men work for him building houses. He also has an office where ten people work. However, the way that he has become successful has made lots of people hate him. Phillip does not care about other people, thinks Susan. He is a man who only cares about himself. He does not let anyone or anything stand in his way. He never cares or *worries* if he *upsets* other people. Not only his *competitors* but also some of his own workers have been the *victims* of his anger and his wish to become rich. She is sure that there are several people in Leeds who do not like Phillip.

"Shall I ring the police?" she asks. "We should let them know that we have *received* another letter."

"No," replies Phillip *sharply*. "I'll call in on my way to the office. I want to know exactly what they have done so far. I don't think that they are really taking it *seriously*."

"I'm sure they are," answers Susan, in an *attempt* to *calm* him. She can hear the *tension* in his voice. She does not want him to drive off down the road in such an angry *mood*. "I think the problem is that they don't have a lot of information to work on. It would help if you had some idea who is sending the letters."

Phillip *shrugs his shoulders* in answer. He finishes his cup of tea and then walks to the door.

"I should be home at about six o'clock," he calls back to Susan. "That is, if this *madman* doesn't kill me first," he says, and he holds the letter in the air.

Susan watches him drive off down the road. At least he has still got a sense of humour, she thinks.

Übung 2: Wie heißt das Wort auf Englisch? Übersetzen Sie!

1. Beweismaterial ____________________
2. Irrer ____________________
3. Anspannung ____________________
4. kleben ____________________
5. wichtig ____________________
6. bekommen ____________________
7. Opfer ____________________
8. Versuch ____________________
9. sofort ____________________
10. Briefumschlag ____________________

It is only two miles to Westwood Police Station but the journey takes twenty minutes. Thousands of cars are driving into Leeds and Phillip can only drive slowly. It is the same every morning, and every morning it makes him angry. He often says that he will leave home earlier in order to *avoid* all the traffic, but he does not like getting up early.

At last he arrives at the police station and finds a space to park his car. It is still raining quite heavily, so he runs to the main door of the police station.

"I would like to speak to Detective Inspector Rush, please," Phillip says to the policeman behind the desk.

"I'll see if he is in, sir. Could I have your name please?" asks the policeman as he picks up the telephone on the desk.

"Tell him it's Phillip Hanson," Phillip says. "And tell him that I

have *received* another letter today. He'll understand."
Phillip stands and watches as the constable repeats his message into the telephone.
"Right," says the policeman into the telephone and then *hangs up*. "Would you take a seat, please, Mr Hanson. DI Rush will be with you as soon as he is free."
Phillip walks towards the seats against the wall, but does not sit down. Instead, he stands and looks out of the window into the police car park. He watches the rain as it falls onto the rows of cars. There will not be much work done on any of the *building sites* this morning. I will be paying men to sit around, drink tea and play cards, he thinks. The sound of someone calling his name brings his thoughts back to the present. He turns and sees that DI Rush is standing in the *doorway* at the side of the desk.

Detective Inspector David Rush has given twenty-five years of his life to the police service. Ten years ago, his wife left him because he worked too many hours. He loves his work more than anything else in his life. *Apart from* his daughter, of course. Sally is a young woman now. He sometimes wishes that they could have spent more time together when she was young. Police work, however, has not given him much time for a private life.

ÜBUNG 3 !

Übung 3: Welches Wort ist das „schwarze Schaf"? Unterstreichen Sie das nicht in die Reihe passende Wort!

1. wife, children, daughter, husband
2. kitchen, hall, door, bedroom
3. say, think, ask, answer
4. face, mood, hand, head

5. emotion, happy, unhappy, angry
6. letter, handwriting, envelope, building site

He is not looking forward to his meeting with Phillip Hanson. Mr Hanson is not the kind of man that anyone looks forward to meeting, the detective thinks. He is one of those people who always seem to be unhappy and angry. It does not *surprise* him that Phillip Hanson is *receiving threatening* letters. The only thing the inspector finds *surprising* is that Mr Hanson has not *received* them more often.

DI Rush holds open the door for Mr Hanson.

"Good morning, Mr Hanson," he says and holds out his hand.

"There's nothing good about it," *complains* Phillip, as he *shakes* the detective's hand. "I've had another letter."

"Yes, I was told that," answers DI Rush, as they make their way down the corridor towards his office.

"Have you opened it?" he asks.

"Yes," replies Phillip. "It's been made in the same way as the others. The same three words as well. 'You will die,' it says. You would think that whoever is sending them would change the message a little bit."

"Yes," agrees DI Rush. "It doesn't give us much to work on. Most *threatening* letters are longer. That sometimes gives us a better idea of the type of person we are looking for."

They enter the office and DI Rush asks Phillip to sit down. He then opens a *drawer* in his desk and takes out a brown *folder*. He lays the *folder* in front of him on the desk, opens it and begins to look through the papers in it.

"Have you thought of anyone who could be sending these letters?" he asks, without looking up from the papers.

"No one *apart from* those people on the list I gave you last week,"

replies Phillip. "They're all people who don't like me. I don't think any of them would go this far, though."
"We've *researched* the list of names. Although you say that they all dislike you, we cannot find any *evidence* that one of them has sent the letters. We can't *interview* them without more *evidence*. Are there any of them who you really think could be sending the letters?" asks DI Rush.
"No," replies Mr Hanson. "I've had problems with all of them in the past, but I don't think that any of them want to kill me."

ÜBUNG 4 !

Übung 4: Lesen Sie weiter und unterstreichen Sie im folgenden Abschnitt die richtige Übersetzung der Wörter in Klammern! ***(Handschuhe, Klebstoff, Briefmarke, Briefumschlag, Blatt, Schreibtisch)***

DI Rush takes a sheet of paper from the *folder*. He looks at it as he continues to speak. "The *forensic science laboratory* hasn't found anything either. The only *fingerprints* on the letters and envelopes are from you and your wife. The man or woman who sent them wore *gloves*. They have used water to wet the *glue* on the stamp and the envelope. Because of that there is no DNA. The only thing we can definitely say is that the letters were posted in Leeds," he *adds*, as he places the sheet of paper back on his desk.
"So where do we go from here?" asks Phillip angrily. "Do we just wait until someone tries to kill me? It will be a little late for me then, when I'm in the *mortuary*."

"We'll talk about what we can do in a moment, Mr Hanson," DI Rush answers *calmly*. "Do you have the letter you *received* this morning? I'd like to take a look at it."

He takes out a pair of plastic *gloves* from a desk *drawer* and puts them on. He then takes the envelope that Phillip holds out to him. He *examines* the writing of the address, and then *carefully* pulls out the letter. He opens it out on the top of the papers in front of him.

"As you said, Mr Hanson, it's just like the other two," he says. "I don't think that we will find anything new here."

"So what are you going to do?" Phillip asks *impatiently*.

"In my *experience*, Mr Hanson," DI Rush begins, "people who send letters like these do so just to *frighten* their *victims*. They have no *intention* of *carrying out* their threats."

Phillip opens his mouth to say something, but the detective holds up his hand. "Please let me finish, Mr Hanson," he says and when Phillip relaxes again, he continues. "However, you are *obviously* taking these threats very *seriously*. Therefore, I think that it would be a good idea to put a personal alarm in your home. When you press it, it sends out a radio signal which goes *straight* to the police *control room*. They will then *immediately* send a police car to your home. I will also give you an alarm to carry with you when you are away from the house. Are you happy with that?"

"I can't really ask for any more," replies Phillip, but he is not happy. "I know that you don't have enough men to give me my own body-guard."

"That's true, Mr Hanson," agrees DI Rush. "Right, I'll send this letter off to the *forensic science laboratory*. You never know. We might be lucky. A *fingerprint* or DNA would certainly help us. And someone will phone you to arrange a time when they can come with the alarm." He pushes back his chair as he stands up. "Unless there is anything else, I'll take you back to the *reception*."

"No, there's nothing else," replies Phillip. "I just hope that this does not become a *murder case*, with me as the *victim*," he *adds sourly*, as he turns towards the door.

Although a week has passed since the arrival of the last *threatening* letter, Susan still feels *nervous* as the post arrives each morning. She is always afraid of seeing the handwriting again. She is *relieved* to find that all she holds in her hand are business letters, bills and the usual *junk mail*. She carries it all through to the kitchen, where Phillip is finishing his breakfast.

"Nothing exciting this morning," she says, as she places the *pile* of envelopes in front of him on the table. "Can you please *tidy up* when you have finished?" she asks. "I'm going to be late if I don't go now."

Phillip *grunts* something which sounds like "Yes" and she goes to the front door. He has not wished me good luck, she thinks. She is going for her first *job interview* in over twenty years and for her it is an exciting *experience*.

ÜBUNG 5 !

Übung 5: Lesen Sie weiter und setzen Sie das richtige Wort ein!
(course, work, education, answered, stand, need, unhappy, children, earn, money)

For Phillip it is different. He has never wanted her to (1.) __________. As soon as he had (2.) __________ in the bank, he wanted her to stay at home as a housewife. They planned to have (3.) __________, but it never happened. *Eventually*, she became (4.) __________ with her life and started looking for a job. Phillip did not want her to do that, of (5.) __________. "What do you (6.) __________ to work for?" he said, when she first told him of her plans. "I (7.) ______________ enough money for both of us."

"That doesn't matter, Phillip," she (8.) ______________. She did not like to argue with him, but she felt she now had to (9.) ______________ up for her rights. "It's not about money. It's about me and my life. I'm lonely and bored here at home every day. I have a good (10.) ______________ and I feel that I should use it."

But Phillip didn't give her any *encouragement*. "Do as you please," he shouted and he walked away angrily.

Susan decided that she would like to work at a school. If I can't have my own children, then I'll spend my time with other people's children, she thinks. She has looked in the newspapers each week and has written to several schools. This morning she is going for a *job interview* at the local junior school. They need a teaching assistant. She gets into her car and turns the key to start it, but nothing happens. Once again, she turns the key but it is the same. She does not normally have problems like this. It is, however, a *damp* morning and perhaps that is the *reason* why the engine will not start. Why today, she thinks. I don't want to be late for my *job interview*. That won't make a good *impression*.

She climbs out of the car, *slams* the door behind her and hurries back into the house.

"The car won't start, Phillip," she says and throws the keys onto the kitchen table.

"What do you want me to do about it?" he asks in a most unhelpful way. He does not even look up from the newspaper as he drinks his tea and still finishes his breakfast.

"I haven't time to call the garage. May I borrow your car?" *begs* Susan. "You can ask one of the men to collect you and take you to the office." She does not like having to *beg*, but she has no *choice*. Even if she calls a taxi, she will still arrive late.

"Okay, if it's so important to you," Phillip replies coldly. "The keys are in my jacket pocket."

"Thanks," Susan calls over her shoulder as she runs into the *hall*, where his jacket is on a hook. With his car keys in her hand, she hurries from the house a second time.

She settles herself in the comfortable seat of Phillip's Mercedes and puts the key into the *ignition*.

The explosion, when she turns the key, breaks the house windows and the car becomes a ball of fire. Phillip runs from the house into the drive. At the same time, people run from the road towards the car. Phillip tries to go near the car, but he cannot because of the flames. "No!" he *screams* and falls to his knees. "Susan!" He holds his head in his hands and his shoulders *shake* as he begins to *sob*. He can do nothing, only watch the *burning* car.

Chapter 2: The Killer Strikes Again

"Take your time, Mr Hanson," says DI Rush. "I know that this is difficult for you, but it is important. We need every bit of information to help us catch your wife's killer."

He looks at the man in front of him. He does not look like the arrogant Phillip Hanson of the *previous* week. Now he is red-eyed and has not shaved. The doctor has given him something to help him to sleep, but he looks as though he has not slept for some time.

Übung 6: Lesen Sie weiter und unterstreichen Sie alle zehn Verben im folgenden Abschnitt!

"If you can just tell us what happened yesterday morning. Start at the time that you got up," continues DI Rush. He *indicates* the officer next to him. "Sergeant Robertshaw will take notes at first. Then we will go through the story again and write everything down."

Phillip slowly begins to tell them how he and Susan got up and ate breakfast together. There are tears in his eyes and he finds it hard to speak. He tells them how happy she was about the *job interview*. "I feel awful now," he says. "I just wanted her to stay at home. I didn't want people to think that my wife had to work."
DI Rush gives him a *tissue* from a box on the desk. Phillip *blows his nose* loudly and then continues.
"When her car did not start and she asked to borrow mine, I never thought anything about it. I just told her to take the keys. I was sitting in the kitchen when I heard the explosion. For a minute, I didn't move. I didn't know what it could be. I thought it was a gas explosion. As soon as I got outside and saw the car, I knew that the bomb was for me. Poor Susan died in my place. Just because her car didn't start."
"It certainly seems that way," agrees DI Rush. "It *appears* that I *underestimated* the threats you *received*, Mr Hanson. Nothing like this has ever happened before."
"Yes," *snarls* Phillip angrily. "Susan would still be alive today if you were good at your job. Perhaps now you will *believe* these threats. Now that it's too late!"
"I realize that you are angry, Mr Hanson, and I understand that you think that the police could have done more. I did all that was possible with the *evidence* that we had," says the detective *calmly*.

"That may be true, but now you have to do even more," says Phillip. "I want you to catch my wife's killer. I want to see him die in *prison*."

"An *incident room* has been opened and we have begun the *investigation* already," DI Rush replies. "Detective Superintendent Whipple is leading the *enquiry*. However, we agree with you. We *believe* that the bomb was in the car to kill you and not your wife. Therefore, we think that the killer will try again. I have to keep you alive, Mr Hanson."

"In that *case*, it would be a good idea if I made my *will*," says Phillip *sarcastically*.

"As from now, we will provide a policeman who will guard you *around the clock*. He will make sure that nothing happens to you," *explains* DI Rush.

Übung 7: Beantworten Sie die Fragen zum Text!

1. How many threatening letters has Phillip received?

2. Who brings the letters to the house?

3. Why should Phillip get up early?

4. How many years has DI Rush been in the police?

5. What has Phillip Hanson given to the police?

6. Why does Susan want her husband's car?

"Now let's go through what we know so far," says Detective Superintendent Whipple. Around the table sit several of the detectives who are *investigating* the *murder* of Susan Hanson. "Would you like to start, Dave?" he says to DI Rush.

DI Rush opens the *folder* in front of him. "Well, sir," he replies, as he looks at the first sheet, "it is now ten weeks since the *murder*, but we still do not have any idea who the *murderer* is. There are lots of people who do not like Mr Hanson. He has made several enemies. In fact, no one seems to like him. When he *received* the first letter, he gave me a list of all the people who might be sending them. We have *checked* all the people on that list. *Apart from* one, none of them can be the *murderer*. The one that we are still looking at is a *joiner* called Jack Wise. Sergeant Robertshaw, can you tell us about Jack Wise, please?"

DS Robertshaw, who is sitting at the end of the table, begins to speak. "Two years ago, Mr Wise did a large amount of work for Mr Hanson on one of his building jobs. Mr Hanson said the work was not good enough and would not pay him. Mr Wise went to *court* and in the end he got his money. However, he almost lost his business and he was very ill. There is another thing which makes Mr Wise of interest to us," continues the sergeant. "He worked at Marshall's *quarry* when he was younger. He used *explosives* there. We have *interviewed* him twice now. He says that he hates Mr Hanson, but that he does not want to kill him. He *claims* that he knows nothing about the letters. However, he was alone on the evening and night before the death of Mrs Hanson. He could have made the bomb and put it in Hanson's car."

"So, Mr Wise is the most interesting of all the people that we have spoken to so far," agrees the superintendent. "Do we know anything further about the last letter? The one Hanson *received* after his wife's death that said 'You will not be so lucky next time'. Could that have come from Wise?"

One of the other detectives speaks. "I'm afraid there's nothing new there, sir. We did not find any *forensic evidence* on the letters. As far as we can tell, each letter was posted in a different area of the city."

"At least the killer has not tried to kill Mr Hanson again," says the superintendent.

"Probably the fact that he has a policeman with him twenty-four hours each day is the *reason* for his good health," replies DI Rush.

"I don't know how long we can carry on though. It is very expensive to have a detective with him every hour of the day and night. What do you think, Paul?" says the superintendent.

A thin, young detective inspector, who is sitting next to DI Rush, answers.

"As you say, sir, no one has tried to kill Mr Hanson in the past ten weeks. However, Mr Hanson *complains* that he cannot do his work because there is always someone with him. He wants us to *protect* him at night but not during the day. Perhaps it's a good time to *reduce* the number of hours that a detective is with him."

"Right," says the superintendent. "Well, I spoke to the *Chief Constable* yesterday. He wants me to cut our costs. Therefore, I am going to *reduce* the number of men on the *enquiry* next week. Unless there is some new *evidence*, of course. Are you going to see Mr Hanson this morning, Dave?" he asks DI Rush.

"Yes, sir. I told him that I would call to speak to him after the meeting," replies the inspector.
"Could you speak to him about the *protection*, then?" asks the superintendent. "I think that he will be happy for us to *reduce* it during the day. Right," he continues, "do we know any more about the bomb?"
Another detective answers. "No, sir. The *forensic* report says that the bomb is *home-made*. *Apparently*, if you know a little bit about *chemistry*, you can easily make one. Mrs Hanson had little chance of *survival*. The bomb was with a can of petrol under the driver's seat."
"Okay," says the superintendent. "Sergeant Robertshaw, I would like you to concentrate on Mr Wise, as he seems to be our only real *suspect* at the moment. Since we are not *protecting* Mr Hanson during the day, I want you to watch Mr Wise during that time. If he is the killer, he may try again when he finds out that there is no longer a detective with Mr Hanson."
"Okay, sir," replies the sergeant and closes his *folder*. "I shall inform you as soon as we know anything."
"Please do that, Sergeant Robertshaw," replies the superintendent. "Right, I have nothing further to ask. Has anyone else anything to *add*?"
When no one speaks, he continues. "Right, gentlemen, let's get back to work. We need to catch this killer."

Übung 8: Wie lautet die Berufsbezeichnung auf Englisch? Übersetzen Sie!

ÜBUNG 8 !

1. Briefträger ____________________

2. Lehrer ____________________

3. Baumeister ____________________

4. Polizist ____________________

5. Tischler ____________________

6. Metzger ____________________

7. Hausfrau ____________________

Before he leaves the police station, DI Rush discusses with DS Robertshaw how they can *obtain* more information about Jack Wise. It is *surprising* what can be found out about a person these days, thinks DI Rush. When I joined the police, there were no computers in the police station. Now, however, we can get *details* of where people have used their credit card, and what they have bought with it. We can *obtain* their mobile phone bills. On these we can see who they call, when they call them, and where they are when they make the call. Also, cameras in the streets can record someone's *movements* minute by minute. With all the technology we have now, thinks DI Rush, we should be able to find out if Mr Wise is the killer or not.

He then makes his way to the offices of Hanson Construction. They are in Headingley, about one mile from the police station. When he enters the building, he sees one of the detectives from the station in the *reception*. As DI Rush comes in, the detective puts down the newspaper that he is reading and stands up.
"Good morning, sir," he calls happily to the inspector, a smile on his face. "How are you?"
"Very well, thank you, Colin," answers the inspector and smiles as well. "Anything to report?"
"No, sir. Another quiet morning. Mr Hanson is in his office. I think

that the *murderer* knows that we are *protecting* him. Nothing *suspicious* has happened at all."

"I have just come to speak to Mr Hanson. He wants to *remove* the *protection* during the day. What do you think, Colin?" asks the DI.

"I don't think the *murderer* will *strike* again while we are with Mr Hanson, sir. The question is, how long can we *protect* him? We can't do it for the rest of his life. It has to stop sometime," replies the detective and *shrugs his shoulders*.

Übung 9: Lesen Sie weiter und ordnen Sie die Buchstaben in Klammern zu einem sinnvollen Wort!

ÜBUNG 9 !

DI Rush (1. kaepss) ________________ to the *receptionist* and then walks towards the offices. He knows his way to Mr Hanson's (2. cefofi) ________________. Since the (3. redrum) ________________ of Mrs Hanson, he has visited almost daily. He (4. skkonc) ________________ on the door.

"Come in, Inspector," calls Mr Hanson's voice. The (5. sitpeerconit) ________________ has *obviously* phoned him, thinks DI Rush. Mr Hanson is seated behind his (6. sked) ________________, which faces the door. "Any news for me?" he asks, as the (7. rotnspice) ________________ enters the room.

"Good morning, Mr Hanson," answers DI Rush and thinks once again how *impolite* Hanson is. "How are you?"

"Yes, yes, I'm fine. Never mind that," says Hanson *impatiently*. "Do you have any news about my wife's killer? Over two months have passed since she died."

"Do you *remember* the list of names that you gave me when you *received* your first letter?" asks the inspector.

Hanson nods.

"One of the men on the list is very interesting to us," continues the inspector. "A man called Jack Wise."

"Jack Wise," laughs Mr Hanson. "He's not big enough to *frighten* anyone."

"You don't need muscles to make a bomb," replies the inspector. "He used to work at Marshall's *quarry*. He used *explosives* there. Also, he has no alibi for the night before your wife's death. It could easily be him."

"Perhaps you're right, Inspector," agrees Mr Hanson. "Jack was really angry when he had to go to *court* to get his money. I shall never forget the *hate* in his eyes that day," he laughs.

"Well, from tomorrow, we shall watch him every day," says the inspector.

"He is not likely to try to kill me when I have a detective with me all the time," replies Mr Hanson.

"Well, that is the other *reason* for my visit today. We have decided to agree to your *request*. We are not going to *protect* you during the day."

"Good," says Mr Hanson. "You don't know how difficult it is for me. I am trying to *run* a business with a detective watching me all the time."

"Of course, we realize that," agrees DI Rush. "However, your *safety* is more important than your business."

"Both are important to me," replies Hanson. "Anyway, is there anything else? I'm very *busy*."

"No," answers DI Rush, *surprised* once again at how *impolite* Hanson sometimes can be.

On his way out, the inspector speaks to the detective in the *reception*. "You can come back to the station with me, Colin. Mr Hanson no longer needs *protection* during the day. I'm sure we can find some work that is more interesting for you."
The detective folds his newspaper. He smiles and *gets to his feet*. "*Thank goodness* for that," he laughs. "I have read two newspapers already this morning!" He calls goodbye to the *receptionist* and follows the inspector out of the door.

DI Rush buys a sandwich for lunch and then goes to see Superintendent Whipple.
"Hanson is happy for us to *remove* the *protection* during the day," says the inspector. "I have brought the detective who was with him back to the police station. He is going to work with DS Robertshaw's team."
"Good," answers the superintendent. "I was just thinking…"
At that moment, the telephone on the desk rings. The superintendent picks it up and listens for a few moments. "Right," he says. "DI Rush and I are on our way to the *crime scene* now."
He puts down the telephone, a *grim* expression on his face.
"Well, Dave, we were certainly looking at the right *suspect*," he says.
"Why? What's happened?" asks the DI.
"That was the *control room*," the superintendent continues. "*Apparently*, Jack Wise has just been to Phillip Hanson's house and has attacked him with a knife. There has been a *struggle* and Jack Wise is dead. It seems as though Jack Wise murdered Susan Hanson after all."

Chapter 3: DI Rush Has Doubts

When they arrive at Phillip Hanson's home, they see a uniformed police officer at the side of the road. DI Rush stops the car and speaks to him through the open window. "What's happened?"

ÜBUNG 10

Übung 10: Lesen Sie weiter und finden Sie die Synonyme für die folgenden Ausdrücke im Text!
(1. reach a destination, 2. where the cook works, 3. serious injury, 4. a person who cares for the sick, 5. cutting instrument, 6. fight, 7. lifeless)

"Mr Hanson pressed the alarm in his house. I was the first person to arrive," he tells them. "Mr Hanson was in the kitchen. He was holding a *cloth* to a deep knife *wound* to his face. He also has a cut on his hand. He's gone to hospital as he *obviously* needs to see a doctor. Before he left, he told me that Mr Wise came to his door. As soon as Mr Hanson opened the door, Mr Wise pulled out a knife and attacked him. It looks like there was a *struggle* in the *hall*. That's where Mr Wise's body is. Mr Hanson says that Mr Wise fell on the knife during the *struggle*. The *paramedics* who came for Mr Hanson had a look at Mr Wise as well. They said that there was nothing that they could do for him. He was already dead."

DI Rush drives up to the house and parks the car. Both detectives go to the back door of the house where two police officers are standing.
"Have you two been into the house?" asks the superintendent.
"No, sir, we haven't," *immediately* answers one of them. "We are just here to *protect* the *crime scene*."

“Good,” replies the superintendent. “Don’t let anyone else in without my *permission*.”

Followed by DI Rush, he enters the kitchen and walks through to the *hall*. It certainly looks as though there has been a *struggle*. The small telephone table lies on the floor and the telephone cable hangs from the wall. The curtains have been pulled down and pieces of a large *ornament* are lying all over the floor. There is also lots of blood on the floor and on the walls. In the centre of the *hall* is the body of a man. He is lying face down, a *pool* of blood near his right side.

The superintendent looks at the scene in *silence* for some minutes. “It looks like a *slaughterhouse*,” he says finally. “I don’t think that I have ever seen so much blood.”

“No,” agrees DI Rush. “It certainly seems as though the *struggle* lasted for some time.”

Neither of them enters the *hall*. They do not want to *disturb* the *crime scene* before the arrival of the *forensic* team.

“Speak with the policeman outside, Dave,” says the superintendent. “Tell him that only the doctor and the photographer can come in. Everyone else will have to wait until the *forensic* team have finished. We don’t want anyone to walk on any *evidence*. I’m going back to the *incident room*. I’ll arrange for a team to begin *enquiries* at the neighbours’ houses. Perhaps someone saw Mr Wise arrive.”

“Okay, sir,” answers DI Rush. “What about Mr Hanson? Do you want me to see him at the hospital?”

“Yes, you could do that,” agrees the superintendent. “Just have a talk with him and find out what he has to say. You can take a written *statement* later at the police station. That is, if he is not too badly *injured*.”

When the superintendent has left, DI Rush stands alone in the *silence*. He looks at the body and the blood on the floor and walls.

It seems that the *murder enquiry* is over. Now, all that we have to do is complete the paperwork, he thinks. It looks as though Jack Wise killed Susan Hanson and then tried to kill Phillip Hanson. There will not be a *trial*. Phillip Hanson was only *protecting* himself.

! ÜBUNG 11

Übung 11: Lesen Sie weiter und unterstreichen Sie im folgenden Abschnitt die Übersetzung der Substantive in Klammern!
(1. Krankenhaus, 2. Gesicht, 3. Bauunternehmer, 4. Tod, 5. Polizist, 6. Polizeirevier)

DI Rush arrives at the hospital as Phillip Hanson is leaving. He has a large *dressing* on the left side of his face and a *bandage* covers most of his right hand. He sees the detective in the corridor.
"Ah. The police. Too late again, Inspector," he says. "It's a good thing that I can look after myself."
"Mr Hanson," replies the inspector, "we stopped guarding you during the day because you asked us to do so."
The two men are now facing each other. The builder does not reply. He just looks at DI Rush angrily.
"I need to speak to you about the death of Mr Wise," continues DI Rush.
"Can't that wait?" replies Mr Hanson. "I'm *injured*. Anyway, I have already told the whole story to the policeman who came to the house."
"Well, I want to hear it from you, Mr Hanson," *insists* DI Rush. "Do you want to speak to me here, or do you want to come to the police station?"

Mr Hanson *scowls*. "I'll speak to you here, if I must," he *growls*. DI Rush asks if he can use one of the doctors' offices. When they are both seated, he takes out a notebook and his pen. "Right, Mr Hanson," he begins. "Could you please tell me what happened this lunchtime? I shall make a few notes while you are talking."

Mr Hanson then tells the inspector what happened. He says that he decided to go home for his lunch. He was in the house for about ten minutes when the doorbell rang.

"I opened the door. Jack Wise was standing there. I was *immediately worried*. You told me this morning that he was the *suspect* for sending the letters and killing Susan. I said to him, 'What do you want?' and he replied, 'You.' He pulled his hand out of his pocket. I saw that he was holding a large knife. He tried to *slash* my throat. I moved out of the way and put up my left arm to *protect* my face, but he was still able to cut my cheek. As you can see," he says and he *points* to the *dressing* on the left side of his face. "He came after me, *slashing* at me. I tried to *grab* the knife, but it was really *sharp*. It cut my hand open. I have a deep cut across my hand." He holds up his *bandaged* hand to show DI Rush. "*Eventually*, I managed to *grab* his *wrist*. That's when we fell over the telephone table. He went down first with me on top of him. I heard him cry out and then he was still. I *got to my feet* and he didn't move. I saw that the knife was in his *chest*." He stops and thinks for a moment and then continues.

"I knew that he was bitter, but I never thought that he hated me so much." He stops again for a few moments. "Then I went into the kitchen and pressed the alarm. It was only a few minutes before the first police car arrived."

"Thank you for that, Mr Hanson," says DI Rush. "I'll leave you alone now. *Obviously*, I want to speak to you again and to take a written *statement* from you. I should just tell you that you will not be able to go home until the *forensic* team has *examined* the house. Do you have somewhere to stay for the night?"

"I can probably stay with my sister. She lives in Chapeltown," answers the builder.
"Please ring the *incident room* and let us know where you are," calls the inspector as Mr Hanson walks away.

ÜBUNG 12

Übung 12: Wie heißt das Verb im Simple Past?

1. nod	______	6. shut	______
2. die	______	7. find	______
3. think	______	8. examine	______
4. see	______	9. take	______
5. tell	______	10. can	______

Two days later, DI Rush is not happy. "I know that we found one of the *threatening* letters in Jack Wise's pocket, sir. However, I just have a feeling that there is something not right," he *explains* to Superintendent Whipple. "I don't know why, but I do not *believe* that we have discovered the truth. Everything just seems to be a little too…" He pauses and tries to think of the correct word. "I think '*convenient*' is the best word to describe it, sir. The fact that Jack Wise arrived at Hanson's house only hours after I told Hanson that he was our main *suspect*. Also, the fact that he had one of the letters in his pocket. What do you think?"
"I have thought about it, Dave," answers the superintendent. "However, there is no *evidence* against Mr Hanson. I don't like him either, but that doesn't make him a *murderer*. As far as we know, he and his wife were happy together. Her friends say that he never *threatened* her. Also, he had no *reason* to kill her that we know of.

There was no other woman in his life. I'm sorry, Dave," says the superintendent, "but I think that you're wrong. You will just have to accept that Jack Wise was the *murderer*. Look at the *evidence*. He had another letter in his pocket and he tried to kill Hanson. He probably came to post the letter *in person,* and when he found Hanson at home without a detective, he decided to attack him. I think that is enough *evidence*."
"Well, sir," replies DI Rush, "I just want you to know what I think."
"That's okay, Dave, but you have to accept the *evidence*," answers the superintendent. "Wise is the *murderer*. Just complete the report. There are other *cases* that I need you to work on."
"Okay, sir. You're the boss," replies the DI.

That lunchtime, DI Rush drives into the city centre to meet his daughter for lunch. He parks his car and walks through the streets to the café. It's a beautiful, sunny day and he *admires* the buildings around him. There are two-hundred-year-old buildings which stand next to new office blocks. DI Rush really likes the mixture of old and new. It's always a pleasure for him to be in the city centre.

Sally is already sitting at a table as the inspector enters the café. She works in a bank in the centre, so they often meet here for lunch. It is the highlight of DI Rush's week. He sees her *waving* and goes over to the table. She stands and they *hug* each other.
"*Hiya*, Dad," she says and they both smile at each other. "How has your day been?" she asks.
He does not often talk about his work, but Sally knows all about the Hanson *case*. It has been in the newspapers every week. It is not every day that someone in the city is killed by a bomb. She also knows about her father's feelings towards Phillip Hanson.
"I have told the superintendent what I think," replies the inspector.

"He *believes* that Jack Wise was the *murderer*. I have to agree that there is no *evidence* against Phillip Hanson. So now I just have to prepare the report," he says and then *adds*, "even though I'm not sure that Wise was the *murderer*."

Sally is very excited. "Well," she says, "I know something which might interest you. I shouldn't really tell you this, I *suppose*. It's against *company* rules to talk about our *customers*. Since this is a *murder*, though, I think I should tell you anyway."

She stops to *breathe*. DI Rush smiles. He thinks how well the name Rush *suits* her. She always speaks as though she is in a *rush*. Her words come out so fast. He often has to tell her to speak more slowly and to *breathe*.

"I was making a cup of tea in the kitchen at work this morning. I heard one of the managers talking about Phillip Hanson. He said that Hanson's *company* is having financial problems. But do you know what? The manager said that Hanson *insured* his wife for one million pounds about six months ago. The *insurance company* have told the bank that they will pay the money into his account in the next few weeks. I think that is a bit *suspicious*. What do you think?"

"A bit *suspicious*! I think it is very *suspicious*," *gasps* the inspector. "You are sure that's what you heard?"

"Yes, definitely," replies Sally.

"It would certainly be a good *reason* for Hanson to murder his wife," says the detective. "If Phillip Hanson sent the letters and put the bomb in the car himself, it *explains* why we didn't find any *evidence* at Wise's house. But if Hanson did kill his wife, why did Jack Wise attack him? That's what I can't understand."

DI Rush wants to get back to the office to look through the *evidence* again, but he tries to drink his coffee and eat his sandwich slowly. He talks with Sally about her work and her life. She is always such a happy girl, he thinks.

When they leave the café, Sally says, "Please don't tell anyone that I told you about Mr Hanson's account."
"No, it will be okay," DI Rush says to her. "We won't *involve* you, Sally."
When he arrives back at the station, DI Rush does not go to the superintendent with the new information. It's not really *proof* of anything. However, he thinks, one million pounds is a good *reason* for Hanson to kill his wife.

Übung 13: Lesen Sie weiter und setzen Sie die richtige Form des Verbs ein!

ÜBUNG 13 !

The following week, DI Rush (1. sit) ________________ in front of the computer every day. He (2. work) ________________ through all the *evidence* that has been (3. collect) ________________. As he is (4. read) ________________ through the report about Jack Wise, there is a knock at the door of his office. DS Robertshaw puts his head around the door. "Have you (5. hear) ________________ the news?" he asks. "Phillip Hanson has (6. sell) ________________ his business."

"Really?" *gasps* DI Rush.
"Yes," continues the sergeant. "He's leaving the country. He's going to *emigrate* to Brazil as soon as the *enquiry* finishes. I thought you would like to know, sir."
"Yes, thanks for that, Steve," replies the inspector. "Thanks very much."
Emigrating, thinks DI Rush. He's certainly not staying around for

long. After a few moments of thought, he returns to the work in front of him. He is reading Jack Wise's medical record. He is about to read the next document, then he suddenly realizes what he has just read. He reads it again: Four weeks before his death Jack Wise cut his right arm at work. Since then he has not been able to use his right hand. DI Rush begins to search the computer system for Phillip Hanson's *statement*. Yes, Phillip Hanson says in his *statement* that Jack Wise held the knife in his right hand. That's why the *wound* was on the left side of his face.

DI Rush thinks for a while. Then he picks up the phone and *dials* DS Robertshaw's number.

"Hello, Steve," he says, when DS Robertshaw answers the call. "I'd like you to *do me a favour*. Did Jack Wise have a mobile phone?"

"Yes, he had," replies DS Robertshaw. "Why?"

"Did you ever look at it to see the calls he made and *received* the day he died?" asks the inspector.

"No, sir," replies DS Robertshaw. "It didn't seem important at the time. The letter in his pocket and the attack on Hanson were enough *proof* that he was the *murderer*."

"Can you *obtain* a list of the calls that he made and *received* on the day he died? As soon as possible, please."

"Okay, sir," answers DS Robertshaw. "I'll do it *right away*."

DI Rush sits back in his chair with a *grim* smile on his face. Off to Brazil, are you, Mr Hanson? he thinks. We'll see about that!

Chapter 4: The Last Call

"I cannot *believe* it, Dave," says Superintendent Whipple, as he looks up from the papers on his desk. "It looks as though you were actually right."

DI Rush tries to *hide* his smile of *satisfaction*. “Yes, sir,” he replies. “Not only does the *insurance policy* for one million pounds give Hanson a *motive* for killing his wife, but also Wise’s medical record and the list of his telephone calls *suggest* that Hanson really lied to us.”

“Well done, Dave,” continues the superintendent. “I think we should bring Mr Hanson to the police station for an interview. He has several questions to answer.”

“Very good, sir,” replies the DI. “I’ll be very happy to *arrest* him and *interview* him. If it’s okay with you, I’ll take DS Robertshaw with me. He knows all the *evidence* as well as I do.”

“Yes, do that, Dave,” answers the superintendent. “And keep me informed.”

“Of course I will, sir,” says the DI as he leaves the office, a big smile on his face.

Übung 14: Bringen Sie die Wörter in die richtige Reihenfolge!

1. Hanson emigrate Brazil Mr to going is to

2. police letter pocket the found a Wise’s in

3. police mobile check murdered the the the of man phone

4. arrest inspector Hanson the wants to

The first thing that DI Rush sees as they drive down the road towards Phillip Hanson's house is the large "*For Sale*" sign in the garden.

"He certainly seems to be in a hurry to sell everything and leave," says DS Robertshaw.

"Yes," answers the DI. "He must be *worried* that we'll discover the truth."

They turn into the drive which leads to Hanson's house and park in front of the garage. Both men get out of the car. DI Rush rings the doorbell, but no one comes. He rings again and they wait for a few minutes.

"There's no one in, it seems," says the DI. They walk around the house and look through the windows. In every room there are boxes packed with books, *ornaments* and other things.

"It looks as though he is almost ready to leave," *remarks* Sergeant Robertshaw. "At least we aren't too late."

"Perhaps he is at his office. We'll try there," says DI Rush and they return to the car.

It's almost dark when they park the car in the car park of Hanson Construction. As they *approach* the building, they see Hanson lock the door and begin to walk towards his car. When he sees the two detectives, he stops.

"Inspector Rush. What are you doing here?" he asks, as he tries to *hide* his *surprise*. "Have you come to say goodbye?" he asks, laughing *nervously*.

"I think we need to talk before you leave, Mr Hanson," says the inspector. "I would like you to come to the police station with us."

"Sorry, Inspector. I can't do that. I have several things that I must do before I leave."

"Then, Mr Hanson, I have no *choice*," replies the inspector. "I am

arresting you on *suspicion* of the *murder* of Susan Hanson and Jack Wise."
Hanson laughs, but his face turns *pale*. "Is this a joke, Inspector? Jack Wise murdered my wife. I killed him to *protect* myself."
"It's no joke, Mr Hanson. Now come with us, please."
"You're making a big mistake, Inspector," says Hanson. He sounds *brave*, but DI Rush is *pleased* to see that he is *trembling* as he climbs into their car.

Übung 15: Wie heißt das Verb auf Englisch? Übersetzen Sie!

ÜBUNG 15 !

1. antworten ______	4. beschützen ______
2. töten ______	5. behandeln ______
3. entfernen ______	6. auswandern ______

Phillip Hanson sits in the interview room with his *solicitor*, facing DI Rush and DS Robertshaw.
"Right," says DI Rush. "I have asked you about the one-million-pound *insurance policy* on your wife's life. You say, quite correctly, that it does not mean that you killed her. In your *statement*, you said that Jack Wise held the knife in his right hand. That's why the cut was on your left cheek. I have told you that Jack Wise could not have held the knife in his right hand. You now say that you were mistaken. He had the knife in his left hand. Even though he was right-handed."
"If that is all the *evidence* that you have, Inspector," *interrupts* the *solicitor*, "then I *suggest* that you allow Mr Hanson to leave."
"Yes," *adds* Hanson, smiling coldly. "As you know, Inspector, I have things to do before I leave the country."

"Just one more question, Mr Hanson," continues the inspector. "Can you tell me why you rang Jack Wise at two minutes past twelve on the day you killed him?"

The smile *disappears* from Hanson's face and he turns *pale*.

"Really, Inspector," says the *solicitor*. "You should have told me about this before the interview. I shall have to tell Mr Hanson not to answer the question."

"I do not think an answer is really necessary," replies the inspector. "Mr Hanson rang Jack Wise. What he said to him, I don't know, but Mr Wise came to the house. Mr Hanson knew that he was our main *suspect*, didn't you Mr Hanson? I told you so that morning. When Mr Wise arrived, you invited him into the house and *stabbed* him. You then put the letter in his pocket. Afterwards you cut yourself, pressed the alarm and *claimed* that he attacked you. You thought that we would *believe* the story. You did not think that we would *check* Mr Wise's telephone, did you Mr Hanson?"

Phillip Hanson sits and stares at the table and says nothing.

Six months later, DI Rush is in the café with his daughter. "You should have seen Hanson's face when they *found him guilty*," he says. "He *denied* the *murders*. He said he had no idea why his telephone number *appeared* on Jack Wise's telephone. Unfortunately for him, the *jury* did not *believe* him. He is now going to *prison* for twenty-five years."

"The fact that he killed his wife for money is bad enough, but to kill poor Mr Wise to give himself an alibi is really terrible," says Sally. "It's good that there are not many people like Phillip Hanson in the world."

"Indeed it is, Sally," replies the inspector and he smiles at his daughter. "Indeed it is."

MOTIVE FOR MURDER

Alison Romer

Chapter 1: Strangled

Hands are around her neck, slowly pressing the life out of her body. She knows she's going to die. She wants to *scream* but can't. She can't even *breathe*. The world turns black and there's a ringing noise in her ears. The ringing doesn't stop.

Clea *woke up* with a *shock*. She was in her own bed. The clock on the bedside table said 4:26 a.m. Someone was ringing her doorbell. For a moment, she couldn't move. She felt like a swimmer who had nearly *drowned* in deep water. The dream had been so real, death so close. Finally, she *switched on* her bedside light. Her hands went up to her neck as she looked around her bedroom. Everything seemed normal, except for the ringing. Whoever was at her door was still there. Clea had a sudden *rush* of fear. People only rang doorbells or phones so early when it was an *emergency*.
Something terrible has happened, she thought as she jumped out of bed. At the door, she picked up the *entry phone*.
"Hello?" she said. She felt like she was still dreaming.
"Clea, it's us," said her mother's voice. She sounded *strange*.
"Mum? Dad?" Clea asked. "What are you doing here?"
"We have to come in," her father said. "Then we'll tell you."
Clea *immediately* pressed the *buzzer* and opened the door of her flat. She heard her parents come up the stairs. When they arrived, their faces were *pale*. Her mother *immediately* started to cry. Her father's eyes looked full of pain.
"It's your sister," he said. "She's dead."

At that moment, Clea's mother *collapsed*. Together, Clea and her father helped the *elderly* woman to the sofa.

"It can't be true," said Clea. It was like she'd never *woken up*.

It must still be a dream, she thought.

"She was murdered," said her father. His eyes filled with tears. "Our beautiful Tessa was murdered."

ÜBUNG 1

Übung 1: Wie heißt das Simple Past der folgenden unregelmäßigen Verben?

1. ring ____________________
2. come ____________________
3. feel ____________________
4. find ____________________
5. know ____________________
6. leave ____________________
7. make ____________________
8. stand ____________________

That night, Tessa had had a visitor. She'd *poured* two gin and tonics. Both glasses were still full when the police *crime scene* investigators arrived forty minutes later. A neighbour had heard *screaming* at midnight and called the *emergency* number. The police found the gin and tonics, made with lemon and ice. They'd also found Tessa, *strangled* to death, lying on the sofa. Within an hour, journalists and photographers had arrived at the house. Tessa McGowan was a well-known news presenter. She read the big news

stories to thousands of television viewers throughout Scotland. Now her own *murder* was the big news.
Later that day, the police called Clea. They wanted to talk to her. She went on the bus to Pitt Street Police Station. The Glasgow streets looked grey and cold. Clea's head felt light, like a balloon. She took out her mobile phone and looked at Tessa's number. They were not only sisters; they were best friends. They talked every day and told each other everything. Now Tessa would never answer her phone again.

Übung 2: Lesen Sie weiter und setzen Sie die Begriffe in Klammern richtig ein!
(minutes, thank you, feeling, station, everything, officers, desk)

ÜBUNG 2 !

Clea got off the bus. (1.) ____________ she did felt slow. It was like moving through *glue*. Inside the police (2.) ____________, an officer showed her into a small room. It had a (3.) ____________ and three chairs. After a few (4.) ____________, he put his head around the door and asked her if she wanted coffee or tea.
"No (5.) ____________," she said. She hadn't eaten or drunk all day, but she wasn't (6.) ____________ like it at all.
A short while later, two police (7.) ____________ came into the room. They both sat down.

"I'm Detective Inspector Shannon Binlow," said the woman. Then she *switched on* a tape recorder. She said the time and the date.

"I'm sorry about your sister," she said in a *serious* voice.

Clea did not reply.

"Now, Ms McGowan," DI Binlow went on, "what can you tell us about Colin MacDougal?"

"Colin MacDougal?" Clea repeated. "What has he got to do with this?"

"We've *arrested* him for *murder*," DI Binlow said.

Clea looked at her in *shock*. Colin was a married man, but he was having an *affair* with Tessa. It had been going on for more than a year. Clea knew all about Colin. She wasn't happy about the *relationship*, but he wasn't a bad person. In fact, Clea would have liked him if things had been different. Tessa wanted him to leave his wife. He told her he would, but it was taking him a long time to do it.

"Tessa was going to break up with Colin, wasn't she?" the inspector asked.

"Yes, but…" said Tessa.

It was true that her sister wanted to end the *relationship*. The day before the *murder*, Tessa had called Clea.

"I can't go on like this any more," she had said. "I'm going to break up with him tonight when I see him."

DI Binlow looked *serious*.

"That night, she told Colin it was over, and he became angry," she said. "Then he killed her."

"No, I don't *believe* it!" Clea *exclaimed*. "She called me. She was still alive when Colin went home. He could get angry sometimes, but we all do!"

At around 10:30 p.m., Tessa had called her sister again. She told Clea that she hadn't broken up with Colin after all. Instead, he said he would leave his wife soon. Tessa said he was stressed and *upset*, but things were okay between them when he left.

"He didn't go home," said DI Binlow. "He said he drove around in his car for another three hours. He has no alibi. He was the last person to see Tessa alive. *Witnesses* saw him going into the house at 8:30 p.m. The neighbour heard a man shouting at 10:00 p.m. Colin MacDougal has a *motive* for *murder*."

"What *motive*?" Clea asked.

"Your sister wanted him to leave his wife. She *threatened* to end the *affair* if he didn't," Binlow replied. "This made him angry. And he has a police record for violence. In 1985 he was *arrested* for fighting outside a pub. One man was *hurt*."

"But he must have been about eighteen years old!" said Clea. She just couldn't *believe* that Colin was a *murderer*.

"Did he ever *hurt* your sister?" the inspector asked.

"No!" she replied. "He loved Tessa."

"Sometimes people kill the ones they love," DI Binlow said.

When Clea got back from the station, there was a woman standing outside the door. She was holding a big bunch of flowers. It was Valerie Findlay, who had worked with Tessa at the television studio. She was a reporter.

"I was waiting for you," Valerie said. "Can I come in?"

Clea opened the door.

"I'm sorry, I'm not really in the *mood* for visitors," she replied.

"It's just so terrible!" Valerie *exclaimed*. "I can't *believe* it's happened!" She gave the flowers to Clea.

"Thanks," said Clea, "but I can't invite you in. I really need to be alone right now."

"I understand," said Valerie. "If you need to talk, please come and find me. Tessa was so clever, so beautiful. She was a wonderful person..."

"Sorry," Clea *interrupted*. "I have to go."

She went inside and shut the door, leaving Valerie on the step. As she walked up the stairs, she felt bad. The woman was only trying to help. She'd worked closely with Tessa.
I'll call her later in the week, Clea thought.

Back inside her flat, she realized that she had many telephone messages. She listened to some of them: Martin McCray, who read the news with Tessa, a few old friends, a cousin in Edinburgh. There were even some from the *adult education college* where she worked. She taught art classes there. Some of her colleagues had called. Everyone wanted to say how sorry they were.
She put down the phone and went to sit on the sofa. On the bookshelf was a photo of the two sisters. They'd gone on holiday to Florence together five years ago. The photo showed them smiling, with the *gorgeous* city in the *background*.

ÜBUNG 3 !

Übung 3: Lesen Sie weiter und unterstreichen Sie die richtige Variante!

Clea started to feel angry. Someone had (1.) taked/taken Tessa's life away. Was it Colin? The police (2.) needed/needs to make an *arrest* quickly. Tessa was a famous *news anchor*, so (3.) anyone/everyone was interested in the *murder*. It would look good for the police if they *immediately* (4.) found/finded the killer. Clea thought about the last few weeks and about (5.) all things/everything that Tessa had said about Colin.

He wasn't exactly a 'good guy', because he had a wife and a girlfriend at the same time. But Colin as a *murderer* didn't seem right. Suddenly, she *remembered* something. One week ago, the sisters

had met for coffee in a café. Tessa had been happy.
"I've found a big news story!" she had *exclaimed*. "I've got some explosive information."
Clea asked for more *details*. Tessa said she'd have to wait and see.
"Some people would kill for this information," she said. "I can't tell anybody yet. Not even you, Clea!"

Clea jumped up and picked up the phone. She called police headquarters and asked for DI Binlow. When the inspector answered, Clea told her about Tessa's information. Binlow was not really interested. The police *believed* that Colin MacDougal was *guilty*. That was the end of the story.
"Can I see him?" Clea asked the detective.
"You can apply for *prison* visit papers," Binlow said. "But it will take some time. I know it's hard for you to *believe*, but MacDougal killed your sister. Don't go to see him. It'll only *upset* you. Perhaps you'd like to contact our *victim counselling* service?"
Clea thanked her and *hung up*. She wanted to hear Colin's side of the story first. She knew that people in *prison* could get letters. They could send them too. She went to her desk and got some paper and a pen. Then she began to write.

> Colin,
> I can't *believe* that you killed Tessa. Please tell me it wasn't you. We don't know each other, but I have a lot of *reasons* to hate you. You had an *affair* with my sister. You didn't care about your own wife. But I think you are *innocent* of the *murder*. I need to know what really happened to Tessa. Please write to me and tell me the truth!
> Clea McGowan.

That afternoon, she took the letter to the *prison*. She hoped Colin would write back soon. Then she went to Tessa's house to start packing her sister's things. Her father and mother did not want to go. Her mother had gone to the doctor's for some tablets because she couldn't sleep. When she thought of Tessa's *murder*, she *collapsed*. She couldn't go out or *switch on* the TV. The newspapers and the news always had stories about the *murder*, and Tessa's photo was everywhere. It was hard enough planning the *funeral*, so Clea said she would go to Tessa's. Her parents wanted her to pack Tessa's books and jewellery.

ÜBUNG 4 !

Übung 4: Übersetzen Sie und enträtseln Sie das Lösungswort!

1. Motiv □ _ _ _ _ _
2. Verdächtiger _ □ _ _ _ _ _
3. Beerdigung _ _ _ _ □ _ _
4. Tod □ _ _ _ _
5. Zeuge _ _ _ _ □ _ _
6. bedrohen _ _ □ _ _ _ _ _
7. Geheimnis _ _ _ _ □ _
8. Affäre _ _ _ _ _ □

Lösung: _ _ _ _ _ _ _ _

The house was in Pollockshields, just outside the city centre. It was a nice, quiet area that had many large houses. Professionals and families lived there. Tessa's house had three bedrooms and a beautiful garden. Inside, the police had finished their *investigation*, and it was as if Tessa had just left. In the bathroom, her face creams and hairbrush were still there. In the bedroom, her pyjamas were lying on the bed. It seemed that Tessa would come through the door at any minute. Together the sisters would cook spaghetti. They would have some red wine and watch a movie. Everything would be normal.

Clea went to Tessa's desk and *switched on* the computer. Tessa's handbag was lying on the desk too. Clea opened it while the computer started. There was a mobile phone, some make-up, keys and an appointment book. Clea opened the appointment book and turned to the date Tessa had died. It said: 'Colin, 8:30 p.m.'
At around 10:30 p.m., Colin had left. The police *believed* that he had come back again. Around midnight, there had been a huge argument. The neighbour had heard Tessa *screaming* and shouting. Clea looked back through the appointments. She saw her own name, the day they met at the café. She kept looking back. Then she saw a *strange* appointment on the 11th. Tessa had written 'M., 11:15 a.m., Starbucks, Buchanan Street.' Next to the information there was a phone number too. The only 'M' Clea could think of was Martin McCray. But why would Tessa meet her colleague at Starbucks? They were together all day anyway. Tessa and Martin went to the television station at 9:00 a.m. in the morning. They worked hard, until 9:00 or 10:00 p.m. Sometimes they would stay even later. So who was 'M'?
Clea turned to the computer. She typed in Tessa's password: George. When they were children, the family had a dog called George. Tessa had really loved him, and always used his name as a password. Clea felt *guilty* about looking at her sister's private papers and emails, but she wanted more information.
The police were happy to have Colin *under arrest*, but it didn't feel right to Clea. Now she had to take on the role of detective.

Übung 5: Lesen Sie weiter und verbessern Sie die falsch geschriebenen Wörter!

She went (1. throu) ______________ Tessa's emails. There were some from Martin, and some from an old (2. universitet) ______________ friend named Maura, both 'M' names. Clea found Maura's number in the (3. apojntment) ______________ book and called her. Maura said she hadn't had a meeting (4. witch) ______________ Tessa on the 11th. She'd seen the news about the *murder* and was very (5. schoked) ______________. Clea told her the *funeral* was in (6. to) ______________ days' time.

After they said goodbye, she went back to the emails. Suddenly she noticed some from Bonnie MacDougal, Colin's wife. It was *strange* that she was writing to Tessa. Clea opened one of the emails. It seemed that Bonnie knew all about the *affair*. Clea was *shocked* to read that Bonnie had *threatened* to come to Tessa's house and *smash* all the windows. In another email, she wrote, "I'm watching you. I know where you live."

Clea *wondered* if the police had seen the messages. She thought of calling DI Binlow again. Had the police seen the *threatening* emails? Had they talked to Bonnie?

What if she killed Tessa? she thought.

There was still the question of the mysterious 'M'. Feeling *confused* and powerless, Clea walked around the house. She picked up some photos and books. Every time she picked something up she wanted to cry. Packing Tessa's things was too hard. It would have to wait until another day. Tessa's *funeral* hadn't even happened yet and it seemed wrong to be putting things in boxes.

Just then, Clea's mobile phone rang. The number didn't look familiar. It was Martin McCray, Tessa's colleague. He started to ask how Clea was feeling, but then began to cry. Clea was *surprised*. Martin was so cool and *calm* when he read the news. He asked Clea if she wanted to meet for coffee. She said she would meet him in a few days, then she told him about 'M'.

"Did you have an appointment with Tessa on the 11th?" she asked him.

"No," Martin replied. "And I don't know who 'M' is. Tessa never said anything about it."

"Did she tell you about her secret information?"

"She told me she had a huge news story," Martin said. "She was going to *research* it and *break the story* at prime time."

"Prime time?" Clea asked.

"That's the time when most people watch TV," Martin told her. "It's about eight o'clock in the evening."

"Did she tell you what the story was about?"

"She said it was totally secret," Martin said. "She wouldn't even tell me! A big, important story is good for the career. I think she hoped to get her own *current affairs show*."

"I need to know what it was," said Clea. "She said people would kill for this information, and now she's dead. She wrote a phone number down next to the name 'M', and I think I'm going to call this person."

"You should go to the police," Martin said.

"The police won't listen to me. They think her boyfriend is *guilty*, but I don't," she said. "There's something *strange* going on here and I want to find out what it is. I want to know who 'M' is."

Chapter 2: Threatened

Clea said goodbye to Martin and put down the phone. She thought about the famous Hitchcock movie called "*Dial* M for *Murder*". Then she picked up the phone again.

ÜBUNG 6

Übung 6: Beantworten Sie folgende Fragen im Simple Past!

1. Who did Clea ask about the secret information?

She asked Martin about the secret information.

2. Where did Clea and Tessa meet?

____

3. What did Tessa hope to get after she broke the story?

____

4. Where did Clea find Tessa's appointment book?

____

5. Which of Tessa's friends did Clea ring?

____

6. Who had written the threatening emails?

____

She *dialled* and heard ringing at the other end. A man answered and said hello. He sounded *nervous*.
"My name is Clea McGowan," Clea said. The man said nothing.
"Hello?" she asked. "Are you still there?"

"I'm still here," he replied finally. "What do you want?"
"I want to know if you had an appointment with my sister Tessa," Clea said. She felt *nervous* herself.
"We met on the 11th," he said. "We were going to meet again on the 15th. I waited at the café for three hours but she never showed up. Then I saw the news. I'm sorry your sister is dead. Goodbye."
"Wait!" Clea shouted down the phone. "Don't *hang up*!"
Suddenly the man's voice became very low. "It's *dangerous* for you to talk to me."
"What do you mean?" she asked. "Who are you? Did you kill my sister?"
"I think my information killed her," he said. "I *believe* they've *arrested* the wrong man."
"What is this information?" Clea asked. "I have to know. Please meet me!"
"The Starbucks on Buchanan Street, tomorrow morning at 9:30," the man said, simply. "I'll be wearing a green *scarf*." Then he *hung up*.
Clea stood for a moment looking at the phone. Meeting this unknown man was a big risk, but she had to know the truth. She made a quick call to Martin. He didn't answer his phone, so she left a message about meeting 'M'.
Then she put on her coat and hat. She picked up Tessa's appointment book and found Colin's address. There were many *motives* for *murder*, and Bonnie MacDougal had one of them: jealousy. If Clea was now a detective, she had to get as many facts as possible.

A short time later, she arrived outside the MacDougal house. She was *shocked* to see news reporters and cameramen outside. They took some photos of her and one even called out her name. They knew she was Tessa's sister. She didn't speak to them. At the front

door she rang the doorbell. A short, thin woman answered it, but only opened the door enough to put her head around it.
“What do you want?” she asked. “I don’t talk to reporters.”
“I’m Tessa’s sister,” Clea replied.
“Go away!” Bonnie suddenly shouted.
She tried to close the door, but Clea put out her foot and held the door open. She heard cameras taking pictures, and *wondered* how it would be reported in the news the next day.
“Let me in, or I’ll tell these news reporters about the emails,” Clea said quietly. She didn’t really want to do that, but she had to get inside somehow.
Finally, Bonnie let Clea in. Before Clea could speak, Bonnie turned around and started to cry.
“I know he didn’t kill your sister,” she said. “I am one hundred per cent sure he didn’t kill her!”

! ÜBUNG 7

Übung 7: Setzen Sie die passenden Synonyme ein!
(freed, real, prison, innocent, saying, guilty)

“I think Colin is (1. not *guilty*) ______________ too,” said Clea, sitting down on the sofa. “The (2. *genuine*) ______________ *murderer* is out there somewhere. Perhaps he, or she, feels (3. at fault) ______________ that an *innocent* man is in (4. jail) ______________. If the real killer *confessed*, Colin would be (5. released) ______________.” She looked at Bonnie *seriously*.
“What are you (6. telling me) ______________?” Bonnie said. “Do you think I did it?”

"You wrote *threatening* emails to Tessa. The police would probably be very interested in those emails."

"I was very angry when I wrote those emails," Bonnie said. "I was so *jealous*. Colin stayed out late. His *behaviour* changed. I wanted to *hurt* your sister, and I hated her, but I didn't kill her!"

Clea stood up.

"Maybe you did," she said. "Maybe you followed Colin to Tessa's house that night. You hear them have an argument. You see Colin leave. You wait a bit, and then ring Tessa's bell. She lets you in because she can see you're *upset*. She makes some drinks and tries to talk with you. But you *threaten* her, you shout at her, then you *strangle* her."

"No!" Bonnie *exclaimed*. "I didn't do it! I was away that night. My friend was getting married and we had a *hen party* in Edinburgh. I have an alibi!"

"You have an excellent *motive* for *murder*! Were you *jealous* enough to kill my sister?" Clea *exclaimed*.

"Get out of my house now!" Bonnie *yelled*. "I'll call the police if you don't go!"

Clea didn't say another word. She went to the front door. As soon as she opened it, she heard cameras. The reporters started shouting. Bonnie shut the door with a loud bang, and Clea *set off* towards the bus stop. The reporters followed her for a while, asking questions. When she didn't answer, they gave up. As Clea got on the bus, she thought about Bonnie. She was a small, thin woman, but anger gave people extra strength. She could have *strangled* Tessa. Tessa was dead and Colin was in *prison*. Bonnie had perhaps taken *revenge* on the two people who had *hurt* her.

However, there was the *hen party*. That was a problem. Maybe Bonnie had five or six alibis, or maybe she didn't. Clea decided she would write to Colin again and ask him for the names of Bonnie's friends. Then she would visit the friends, even if she had to use Tessa's car and drive to Edinburgh. The women would *remember* Bonnie at the party. That is, if Bonnie was telling the truth. At the same time, she felt sorry for Bonnie. She had lost her husband first to Tessa, and then to *prison*.

After getting off the bus, she walked up her street. Someone was standing at the door of the house. It was Valerie Findlay again. Clea was not happy to see her. Of course Valerie cared, but Clea just wanted to be alone. Although she was a colleague, Tessa hadn't really liked the woman. They saw each other at parties, but they were never friends, unlike Tessa and Martin.

"Hello, Valerie," said Clea.

"I'm very *worried* about you!" Valerie said. "I spoke to Martin. He told me all about the mysterious man Tessa was meeting for information."

Clea unlocked the door. Together the women went up the stairs to the flat. Once inside, Valerie took off her coat.

"Meeting this man alone is too *dangerous*," she said. "I think someone should go with you."

"I'm fine on my own," Clea replied. "We're meeting at Buchanan Street Starbucks. There'll be lots of people around."

"It's not a game, Clea!" Valerie *exclaimed*. "You're not really a detective. I think Colin MacDougal is the *murderer*, but maybe it was someone else. You can't be sure. I'm going to come with you. He can't *hurt* you if there are two of us."

Clea didn't want Valerie to come, but she was right: it might be *dangerous*. It was better to have a *witness*.

"Okay," she said. "We'll go together. But I want to talk to 'M' alone first. He might be angry that I've brought someone else, but I'll get him to talk to us both."

Übung 8: Was gehört zusammen? Verbinden Sie!

1. ☐ tell	a) an argument
2. ☐ send	b) a scarf
3. ☐ watch	c) a question
4. ☐ have	d) the truth
5. ☐ wear	e) the news
6. ☐ ask	f) an email

The next morning Clea had a quick breakfast. The post arrived. There were a few cards from friends and family. There was also a letter from Colin. As she read it, Clea felt like crying.

> Dear Clea,
> I am so sorry for *hurting* your sister. She wanted me to leave my wife, but I wasn't *brave* enough to. However, I loved Tessa with all my heart. We had an argument that night, but I didn't kill her and that's the truth. I cry every night because she's gone. I tell them over and over I didn't do it. I didn't go home for a long time because I was *upset* and I didn't know what to do. I should have left my wife a long time ago. If I had, Tessa would still be alive. I decided to leave my wife the next day, but now it's too late and Tessa will never know how much I loved her.
> Please *believe* me, Clea, I didn't do it!
> Colin.

Clea *believed* him. She'd been unhappy about the *affair*. Sometimes she had been angry with Colin, and with Tessa too. However, Colin wasn't a bad man; he'd just done the wrong thing. Now Clea had to find out who really killed Tessa. If the police wouldn't start a new *investigation*, Clea would have to do so alone.

Chapter 3: Scared

At 9:25 Valerie and Clea met at Starbucks. Valerie sat at another table. She agreed that Clea would go up to the man alone, and *explain* that she'd brought someone else. Then they would talk to 'M' together. Clea looked around. Right at the back of the café she saw a man with a green *scarf*. He had a brown jacket, dark brown hair, and was wearing glasses. He looked about thirty-five years old. He also seemed *nervous*.

Clea went up to him and introduced herself. Then she sat down.

"I need to know why my sister died," she said. She didn't want to make small talk. "How *dangerous* is this information really?"

"There's a lot of money *at stake*," the man replied. He didn't want small talk either. "Hundreds of millions, maybe even billions of pounds. That kind of money can make people kill."

"Who are you?" Clea asked.

"My name is Marcus," said the man. "I'm a *scientist*."

Clea looked *surprised*. A *scientist*?

"What do you know about Tessa's *murder*?" she asked.

"I feel it's my *fault*," Marcus replied. "I contacted Miss McGowan because I needed to tell somebody about all of this. I'm just a *scientist*, but your sister knew all about news and information. I needed help and thought she was the right one to help me. I knew the information was *dangerous*. Now she's dead. So I'm *guilty* of her *murder*."

"But you didn't kill her," Clea said. "Look, you need to tell me the whole story. I've brought someone with me who can help too."

"What?" Marcus *yelled*. He stood up. "I wanted you to come alone! I think they're watching me. It's very *dangerous*."
"*Calm down*," Clea said. "Valerie is a reporter. She was a colleague of Tessa's."
"If they see me with a reporter, I could end up dead," said Marcus, sitting down again. "So could you."
"Who are you talking about?" asked Clea. "Who are 'they'?"
She was starting to get *worried*. She looked around the room. Perhaps someone was watching them all the time. Alone, she and Marcus could be two friends, but Valerie was on TV. Everyone would *recognize* her.
"If you think this reporter can help, I'll talk to her," said Marcus. "But you're both taking a risk by speaking to me."

Übung 9: Welche Übersetzung stimmt? Kreuzen Sie an!

ÜBUNG 9 !

1. Treffen wir uns am Café?
   a) ☐ Shall we meet each other at the café?
   b) ☐ Shall we meet us at the café?

2. Können Sie bitte mir sagen, wo Starbucks ist?
   a) ☐ Can you please say me where Starbucks is?
   b) ☐ Can you please tell me where Starbucks is?

3. Sie trinken immer Kaffee.
   a) ☐ They drink always coffee.
   b) ☐ They always drink coffee.

Clea looked over to Valerie and made a sign for her to join them. She came over and put out her hand for Marcus to *shake*. Then the three of them sat down together. Valerie had a cup of coffee with her but Clea was too *nervous* to drink anything. She *wondered* how Valerie could be so *calm*.

Marcus told them that he wanted to go to the police, but was too *frightened*.

"The police might not be interested," he said. "Then my life will be in danger because they'll know I went to the police."

"Please tell us everything," said Clea.

"Right from the beginning," Valerie *added*. "Then we can decide what to do."

Marcus opened his *leather* bag and pulled out some documents in a *file*. Then he told them about his job as a *scientist*. A large multi-national *company* wanted to build a *processing plant* just outside Glasgow. The area was famous for its beauty and had lots of different kinds of plants and animals. A *processing plant* might *threaten* the *ecosystem*, so *scientists* had to study the area first. The *research* would show if it was safe to build the *processing plant*. After the *research* was finished, the *government* had the power to say 'yes' or 'no' to the *company*. The *company* paid a team of *scientists* to study the area, and Marcus was one of them.

"These documents show the *results* of the *research*," Marcus said, holding up the *file*. "They were given to the *government*. The *results* are good. The *environment* won't be *threatened* and the *processing plant* will be built. The men who *run the company* will make millions of pounds and there'll be new jobs in the area."

"So what's the problem?" Clea asked. "Why are the documents so *dangerous*?"

Marcus answered very quietly.

"The *results* are false," he said. "The *company* is paying some of the *scientists* in more ways than one. They're paid to do the *research*, and then they're paid extra money to make the *results* false. I found out. I also have other documents which show the real *results* of the *research*. Certain kinds of plants that are important to the *ecosystem* will be *threatened*. It's too *dangerous* to build the *processing plant* there. It would be very bad for the *environment*."

"That's terrible!" Clea *exclaimed*. "How could anyone do that?"

"It's about money," Marcus replied. "I think someone in the *government* is *involved* too. Perhaps the *company* is paying him to help."

"So you contacted Tessa," said Clea. "You wanted her to *break the story*."

"Yes," Marcus said. "I thought everybody should know. I needed the help of a journalist. Tessa was famous and important, so people would listen to her. Tessa and I planned to hire a private detective to follow the men from the *company*. We wanted to follow the *scientists* and the *government* officer too. We needed to get as much extra information as possible. The truth is, lots of people could end up in *prison*."

Übung 10: Lesen Sie weiter und tragen Sie die entgegengesetzten Begriffe in die Lücken ein!
(go, luxury, straight away, threaten, dangerous, end)

"That's why the information is so (1. safe) ______________. There's one big boss of the *company* and he could (2. begin) ______________ up in *prison* himself. He'd lose his (3. poor) ______________ lifestyle. It could (4. help) ______________ the whole *company* internationally. Think of all the money!"

ÜBUNG 10 !

"Why didn't you (5. come) ______________ to the police (6. later) ______________?" asked Clea.

"I thought that a *government* official was *involved*. Also, the *company* boss, Mr Wester, is a multi-millionaire. All that power and money can make documents and even people *disappear*."
"Did you give some documents to Tessa?" Clea asked.
"She had copies, yes," Marcus replied.
"I didn't see them in her desk. I *wonder* where they could be."
Clea thought for a moment about Tessa's *murder*. She imagined the scene. A man phones Tessa that night and says he has information about the *research*. He says he's a *scientist*, someone who knows the real *results*. Like Marcus. At home, Tessa waits for Colin. He arrives and they argue. At around 10:30 p.m. he leaves and drives round and round the streets. He doesn't want to end the *affair* but he doesn't want to *upset* his wife. *Meanwhile*, Tessa's next visitor arrives. The false *scientist*. She's happy to see him because he has more information. But he doesn't help her. Instead, he *strangles* her to death.
"What if Tessa told the *murderer* that you had documents and wanted to make them public?" Clea asked Marcus.
"Maybe she didn't have to," he replied. "Maybe they already knew about me and I led them to her. It would have been easy for them to follow me when I met her here the first time. But I don't really understand why I'm still alive. Every time I go out, or the doorbell rings, I think that my life is over."
"There's only one thing to do," Clea said.
"Yes!" Valerie *exclaimed*. "You must give the information to me."
"No!" Clea and Marcus said at the same time.
"I'll hire a private detective myself, then *break the* news *story*," Valerie said, putting her hand on the documents.

"Tessa was murdered!" Clea said angrily. "Perhaps it was because of this information. Tessa should have gone to the police, and now we have to, Valerie."

"Absolutely," said Marcus. "We'll be safer if we go together. The three of us can't be killed all *at once*."

"The *murderer* has been found," Valerie said. "Colin MacDougal did it! The information won't kill me and I need you to give it to me now!"

Clea and Marcus looked at each other.

Slowly, Clea *shook* her head. "You can't be sure, Valerie."

Suddenly Valerie jumped up out of her chair.

"You will not go to the police!" she shouted. "Someone else will get the story then, and my chance will be gone!"

Everyone in the café looked at her. She sat down again and spoke in a low voice. "I *deserve* it! I should have been *news anchor* already, not Tessa. Now the station needs a new one, and that's going to be me! I'm not going to do boring reports about festivals and lost dogs any more. This information will make my career, so don't stand in my way!"

She quickly picked up the documents from the table, then stood up and ran out of the café. Clea was *shocked*. Valerie had used her to get the information. Her *offer* of help hadn't been real. She couldn't move for a moment, but then jumped up and ran out after Valerie. She saw Valerie run along the street until she found a taxi, then she got into it and drove away. Clea was left standing on the street alone.

A minute later, Marcus came up behind her.

"She only has copies of the documents," he said. "I have the original ones at home."

"We should go to the police together," Clea said. "Valerie's life could be in danger."

She felt like crying. Valerie's bitter words had *upset* her, and she *remembered* what Tessa had said about her colleague.
"She can smile and be sweet to your face. But then, when she turns away, her smile *disappears*."
Marcus put his hand on Clea's arm.
"Let's go to the police *immediately*," he said.

ÜBUNG 11 !

Übung 11: Setzen Sie die Verben ins Present Continuous, um zu zeigen, dass in diesem Moment eine Handlung vollzogen wird!

1. (meet) Clea and Marcus ______________________ in the café.
2. (catch) She ______________________ a taxi on the street.
3. (think) I ______________________ of going to the police.
4. (wait) We ______________________ outside the building.
5. (hit) He ______________________ the ball against the wall.

Chapter 4: Hunted

At Pitt Street Police Station, they asked for Detective Inspector Binlow. She didn't look happy to see Clea again.
"A *witness* saw Colin MacDougal's car near Tessa's house at 11:15 p.m.," Binlow said. "Have you come to tell me he's *innocent*? If so, you're *wasting* your time."
Marcus stepped forward. He told Binlow all about the false *research results*. He told her how Tessa had become *involved*. Then together he and Clea *explained* that Valerie Findlay had run off with the information. The DI was *curious*.

"This *company* has done something totally illegal," she said, "and we have special officers who *deal with* this kind of crime. I'll call them right now. Can you stay here until they've talked to you?"

Clea and Marcus were glad someone was listening to them. Binlow had realized how *serious* it was, although she still didn't *believe* it had anything to do with the *murder*.

"One more thing, Ms McGowan," said Binlow before she left. "You seem to be playing private detective. It's a bad idea. Leave the *investigations* to the police. That's our job."

Clea said nothing. She was happy that Binlow was taking them *seriously*, and that an *investigation* would start. But until the real *murderer* was *arrested*, she would keep searching for *clues*.

Clea and Marcus waited for half an hour. Finally, two other officers came into the room. They wanted to hear the story, and needed to see the original documents. One of the officers said he would go home with Marcus and get them. Clea was free to go, but Marcus was *worried*. He wanted a police officer to go with Clea too.

"Her life could be in danger!" he said.

"We don't know that," said the officer. "But if it makes you feel better, we'll drive by Miss McGowan's house every hour tonight. But until we know you are in *genuine* danger, we can't give you an officer for full-time *protection*. We're really *busy* trying to *deal with* all the crime in this city. I'm sorry, that's just the way it is."

Marcus wrote down his address and phone number and gave them to Clea.

"Please call me every few hours," he said. "I want to know you're okay. If you're *frightened* or need any help, just call or come over to the flat. I'm not very *brave*, but I don't want anything to happen to you."

"Thanks," said Clea. "Here's my address and phone number too. I'm not very *brave* either, but I can call the police!"

ÜBUNG 12

Übung 12: Lesen Sie weiter und ordnen Sie die Buchstaben in Klammern zu einem sinnvollen Wort!

Clea caught a bus home. She thought (1. otabu) ______________ Marcus. Already he felt like a (2. endirf) ______________. The fact was, however, she knew (3. hington) ______________ about him. Was he telling the (4. hturt) ______________? The *research* (5. ucodsment) ______________ looked real, but it would be (6. yesa) ______________ to make those. All you needed was a (7. retpumoc) ______________.

Now she'd given him her address and phone number. He seemed nice and she felt she could *trust* him. But perhaps she was wrong. Now, for some *reason*, she felt *nervous* about going home. At the next stop, near the George the Fifth Bridge, she got off the bus. She took out her mobile phone and Tessa's appointment book, found Valerie's number and *dialled* it. There was no answer. The police said they would contact Valerie *immediately*. Maybe she was with them right now. Clea just had to hope for the best.

She thought about Marcus again. His flat was near Pitt Street Police Station, so it wouldn't take him long to give the documents to the officer. Then what would he do? Would he be safe at home? Could she *trust* him? Marcus said the *scientists* were paid a lot of extra money for giving false *research results*. Was it enough money to kill for? Clea had so many questions and no answers.

She walked along the bridge and looked down at the River Clyde. In wintertime there was always a lot of water, and the river was *flowing* very fast. She stopped on the bridge and looked over. She thought about the times she and Tessa had walked through Glasgow city centre. They had shopped, and gone to cafés and art galleries. Tessa had loved the artist Rennie Mackintosh, so they often went to the café at the Mackintosh gallery. Now Clea was alone. Her sister and best friend was dead.

Suddenly, she heard a loud noise behind her. It sounded like car *tyres*. She looked around and was *shocked* to see a dark car with dark windows had driven right off the street. It was driving up onto the *pedestrian* walkway and was heading *straight* for Clea. She was alone on the bridge, and there was nowhere for her to run.

Clea got up onto the side of the bridge and jumped. She heard the car crash into the side of the bridge. Then the *tyres* made a *screaming* noise as the car pulled away again. Suddenly she was under water. The cold was a huge *shock*. She'd hit the water very hard, so for a moment she was *confused* and her head *hurt*. She couldn't *breathe*.

I'm going to *drown*, she thought.

It took a lot of *effort* to move her arms and legs, but finally she managed to swim upwards towards the air. She managed to get her head above water and take a few deep breaths. Water was in her mouth and nose, and she was almost crying. The river *flowed* so fast it simply pulled her along. She couldn't swim against it. The *riverbank rushed* past on both sides. She tried to swim towards it but she wasn't strong enough to fight the water.

Just then, she saw two people, a man and a woman. They were slowly walking along the *riverbank*. When they saw Clea, they started to shout and *wave* their arms. But the river was too fast. Clea saw the woman take out her mobile phone. Then they were too far away for her to see any more. Buildings went past quickly on each side. The water was cold, too cold. Clea could feel the energy *disappearing* from her body, and the water was pulling her under again. It suddenly seemed easier to simply give up, stop fighting, and go under. Then she thought of her parents. One daughter murdered, the other *drowned*. They would never get over it. She had to make one last *effort*!

ÜBUNG 13 !

Übung 13: Welches Wort passt nicht in die Reihe? Unterstreichen Sie das „schwarze Schaf"!

1. witness, policeman, crime, victim
2. scream, whisper, yell, shout
3. sometimes, often, occasionally, never
4. famous, well-known, prominent, unknown
5. unskilled, clever, smart, intelligent
6. help, worry, assist, aid

There were trees and bushes along the *riverbank*. Using all her strength, Clea tried to swim towards them. She got a little bit closer, and closer still. The *current* wasn't as strong towards the *edge* of the river. It was getting easier to swim. Finally she could reach out her hand towards some bushes that were low down, close to the water. They had no leaves, but they were strong.

With a final *burst* of energy, she pulled herself up out of the water, then fell into the *mud* of the *riverbank*. She turned onto her back, *breathing* quickly. All her energy was gone and she was freezing cold. Her bag was still across her body. She slowly sat up and opened the bag. Everything inside was totally wet. Her mobile phone had stopped working. She looked around, but there were no people. There was a street not far away. She managed to stand up, but her legs were not working properly. It wasn't easy to walk and she felt sick.

On the street a few cars drove past. The drivers saw her but didn't stop. After a few minutes, a truck came along, and Clea was *relieved* to see the driver pull over at the side of the road. He opened the door.
"What happened to you?" he asked, starting to laugh. Then he looked at Clea's face.
"I fell into the river," she said. Her clothes and hair were wet. She was *shaking* with *shock* and cold.
"You don't want to go swimming in the Clyde in winter," said the truck driver. "It's too cold. Summer is better. Do you need a ride?"
Clea said yes, and got into the truck. She knew she should tell the police *immediately* that somebody had tried to kill her. All she could think about, however, was getting home. She wanted a hot shower and dry clothes.

The truck driver took her right to her front door. Clea thanked him.
"Will you be okay?" he asked.
"I think so," she replied. "I just need to get warm."
She went inside. After showering, she put on some clean, warm pyjamas and went into the living room. She was still *shaking* badly. She opened her bag and took out the paper with Marcus's number on it. It was wet, but she could just read the numbers.
She *dialled* his home, but there was no answer. Then she tried his mobile, but all she got was his voicemail. She didn't leave a message.
"Where is he?" she said out loud.
Then she called the police and asked for DI Shannon Binlow. The detective asked her a few questions but Clea couldn't *offer* much help. The car had been dark, with dark windows. She hadn't seen the driver and didn't even know what kind of car it was. Her *memories* were mainly of being in the water, *choking*, not able to

breathe. Binlow said she would come to the house *right away* and told Clea to lock the door until she arrived.
"I'm starting to think you could be right," Binlow said. "Maybe MacDougal is *innocent* after all. *Switch on* your TV."

ÜBUNG 14 !

Übung 14: Lesen Sie weiter und unterstreichen Sie die richtige Variante!

Clea (1.) took/put down the phone and *switched on* her television. The news had just started. Martin, Tessa's (2.) colleague/college, was reading it. The picture showed the police (3.) *arresting/arrested* a businessman who was wearing an expensive suit. They (4.) were taking/taked him to a (5.) weighting/waiting police car. Martin said that the man was Mr Charles Wester. Marcus had talked (6.) about/over Wester that morning! She (7.) tuned/turned up the sound on the TV.

The report said that Wester paid *scientists* for false *research results*. Then the picture changed to show a beautiful *landscape*. There were many tiny plants and animals that played an important role in the *ecosystem* of the area. Martin *explained* that two other *company* managers, a *government* officer and three *scientists* were also being questioned.
"There may be a *connection* with the *murder* of my friend and colleague, Tessa McGowan," Martin said. "Police have started an *investigation*. This could be good news for Colin MacDougal, who is *under arrest* for the *murder*."
Clea felt she could *breathe* again. Maybe the real killer would be found and Colin would be free. She was about to try calling

Marcus again when the doorbell rang. She went to the *entry phone* and picked it up.
"Hello?" she said. She hoped it was either the police or Marcus. Instead, it was Valerie.
"Clea, you have to let me in. It's very important," she said.
"I don't want to talk to you," Clea said. "You used me to get that information. You only thought about your career."
"I'm sorry," said Valerie. "Look, I was wrong to behave that way. But now I really need to see you. Let me in."
"You can come in for a minute," Clea said. "But I'm still very angry."
She pressed the *buzzer* and opened the door of her flat. She heard Valerie come up. When she reached the top of the stairs, Clea was *shocked* to see her face. The woman looked *pale*.
"What's the matter?" Clea asked.
Valerie came through the door and didn't even close it behind her before she started shouting.
"You gave those documents to the police!" she *exclaimed*.
"Yes, we thought…" Clea started to say.
"I told you not to!" Valerie said. "That was my story!"
"Please don't be so *upset*, Valerie," said Clea. "I need to know who killed my sister. Maybe an *innocent* man is in *prison*."
"I don't care about him!" Valerie *yelled*. "That information would have made my career!"
She reached over to the coffee table and picked up a glass *candle-holder*. Then she threw it against the wall, where it *smashed* into tiny pieces. Clea suddenly felt *frightened*.
"Please *calm down*," Clea said.
"I want to be the *news anchor*!" Valerie *screamed*. "I'm sick of watching people like Tessa and Martin get to the top. Tessa was in my way, but I had a chance until you came along, playing detective."

"What do you mean?" Clea asked.

Suddenly Valerie's voice became very soft and quiet. "I thought I was *rid of* you when you went over the bridge."

She came closer to Clea. With every step she took, Clea tried to move away, but Valerie followed her.

"Yes," Valerie went on. "I thought you'd *drowned*."

"You're *crazy*!" Clea *exclaimed*. "You tried to run me over with a car!"

She moved towards the phone, but Valerie saw what she was doing. She picked up the phone and pulled it hard. The *cord* came out of the wall. Then she held the *cord* in both hands.

"Tessa was easy to get *rid of*," Valerie said. "I went to her house late that night. Lucky for me, Colin had just been there too. She made us gin and tonics and told me to *calm down*. But how could I be *calm*? For years I watched her push her way to the top. She *stole* my dream, my career."

"That's not true," said Clea. "Tessa was a wonderful journalist. She worked hard for the *news anchor* job."

"She had everything I wanted. I hated her," Valerie said.

"You killed her," said Clea, finally understanding.

ÜBUNG 15 !

Übung 15: Welche der folgenden Aussagen sind wahr? Markieren Sie mit richtig ✔ oder falsch – !

1. Bonnie was at a hen party on the night of the murder. ☐
2. Marcus got the documents from Tessa's house. ☐
3. Valerie was jealous of Tessa's success. ☐
4. Valerie was driving the car that nearly killed Clea. ☐
5. Clea realized that Marcus was the murderer. ☐

"Yes," Valerie said. "Now you know. But nobody else will ever find out."

She came towards Clea, the phone *cord* still in her hands. Clea found herself *backed-up against* the living room wall. There was no way to get past Valerie. Suddenly the telephone *cord* was around her neck. She was *choking*. She tried to push Valerie away, but the woman was stronger. The world started to go black.

At that very moment Valerie *collapsed*. Clea *immediately* put her hands up to her neck and tried to *breathe* again. Valerie was on the floor and around her head were bits of *smashed pottery*. There was *soil* and some kind of plant too. Clea was *confused*. Then she looked up and saw Marcus.

He was simply standing there, *pale* and *shaking*.

"I hit her on the head with the plant," he said. "I brought it as a gift. I wanted to ask you out for a drink to celebrate. It was lucky that the door was open!"

He was so *shocked* he couldn't help laughing.

"*Good timing*!" said Clea. She almost laughed too. Then she started to cry.

Just then, DI Binlow came through the door. She looked at Clea, at Marcus, and at Valerie on the floor. Valerie was still *unconscious*, with the phone *cord* in her hands and bits of plant, *soil* and *pottery* in her hair.

"This should make a good story," Binlow said. "Who wants to start?"

Abschlusstest

Übung 1: Beantworten Sie diese Fragen zur Geschichte „Blood & Breakfast"!

1. What kind of dog do the Larkins have?

____

2. What does DI Rush hear in the night?

____

3. Where do Sally and her father visit the cathedral?

____

4. Why does DI Rush clean the barn window?

____

5. Where does Sally lock Brutus?

____

6. How much are the Larkins paid for each immigrant?

____

Übung 2: Welche Wörter haben eine ähnliche Bedeutung?

1.	☐ answer	a) kill
2.	☐ grubby	b) pull
3.	☐ carefully	c) fight
4.	☐ drag	d) reply

5. ☐ murder e) dirty
6. ☐ struggle f) cautiously

Übung 3: Übersetzen Sie die Begriffe und enträtseln Sie das Lösungswort!

1. Gefangener ☐ _ _ _ _ _ _ _
2. Draht _ ☐ _ _
3. bewusstlos _ _ _ _ _ ☐ _ _ _ _ _
4. gebraten _ _ _ _ ☐
5. Wahl _ _ ☐ _ _ _
6. ruhig _ _ ☐ _

Lösung: _ _ _ _ _ _

Übung 4: Wie heißt das Simple Past der folgenden Verben?

1. hear ______________
2. walk ______________
3. break ______________
4. drive ______________
5. steal ______________
6. eat ______________
7. happen ______________
8. pay ______________
9. have ______________
10. feel ______________
11. tell ______________
12. glow ______________
13. hit ______________
14. fight ______________
15. do ______________
16. say ______________

Übung 5: Unterstreichen Sie die richtige Variante!

1. The burglar/beggar stole the paintings from the gallery.
2. I was a witness to/for a crime.
3. Michael catched/caught the thief.
4. Can you say me/tell me where the cemetery is?
5. The house looked like/how something from a scary movie.
6. It's my reason/fault the painting was stolen!
7. Lottie felt/fell down the stairs.

Übung 6: Beantworten Sie die Fragen zur Geschichte „Death Wish"!

1. What did Susan Hanson want to be?

____

2. What was under the seat with the bomb?

____

3. Who was the main suspect?

____

4. Why did he hate Phillip Hanson?

____

5. Where does Sally work?

____

6. How much was Susan Hanson's life insured for?

____

Übung 7: Welches Wort ist das „schwarze Schaf"? Unterstreichen Sie!

1. cemetery, church, sea, cottage
2. robber, burglar, thief, murderer
3. inspector, criminal, constable, sergeant
4. worried, frightened, scared, afraid
5. actor, painter, sculptor, photographer
6. peaceful, quiet, unconscious, calm
7. moonlight, starlight, sunlight, torchlight
8. exhibition, filing cabinet, auction house, collection
9. take, hear, see, smell
10. softly, gently, beautifully, quietly
11. happily, sharply, angrily, coldly
12. reply, answer, admire, say
13. happy, angry, good, nice
14. here, finger, face, chest
15. scream, laugh, shout, swear

Übung 8: Enträtseln Sie das Lösungswort!

1. Beweismaterial _ ☐ _ _ _ _ _ _
2. Messer _ _ ☐ _ _
3. Brust ☐ _ _ _ _
4. Kunde _ _ _ ☐ _ _ _ _
5. Fingerabdruck _ ☐ _ _ _ _ _ _ _ _ _
6. Versuch _ _ _ _ ☐ _ _
7. Verdächtiger _ _ ☐ _ _ _ _

Lösung: _ _ _ _ _ _ _

Übung 9: Bilden Sie ein sinnvolles Wort aus den Buchstaben!

1. Clea was sitting in front of the (morptuce) ______________.
2. Susan's car does not (rstta) ______________.
3. Sally's father is a police (nocsirpet) ______________.
4. A (ngnpaiti) ______________ has been stolen from the gallery.
5. Clea's sister has been (eurdmerd) ______________.
6. There is a (ailbuetfu) ______________ view of the sea.
7. He made the bomb (filmshe) ______________.
8. Pendle Lee has an old (meceryet) ______________.

Übung 10: Übersetzen Sie!

1. shouting ______________________
2. story ______________________
3. career ______________________
4. freeze ______________________
5. answering machine ______________________
6. deep ______________________
7. leather bag ______________________
8. have an argument ______________________

9. tell the truth ____________________

10. fall in the river ____________________

Übung 11: Finden Sie das passende Gegenteil und verbinden Sie!

1. ☐ famous	a) hate
2. ☐ wrong	b) far away
3. ☐ guilty	c) together
4. ☐ love	d) unknown
5. ☐ alone	e) innocent
6. ☐ fall asleep	f) right
7. ☐ close	g) wake up

Übung 12: Wie heißt das Präsens der folgenden Verben?

1. felt	____________	6. put	____________
2. tried	____________	7. went	____________
3. began	____________	8. could	____________
4. sat	____________	9. spoke	____________
5. fell	____________	10. saw	____________

Lösungen

Blood and Breakfast

Übung 1: 1. richtig 2. richtig 3. falsch 4. falsch 5. falsch 6. richtig 7. falsch 8. falsch

Übung 2: 1. They have travelled by car. 2. She shakes his hand reluctantly because it is dirty. 3. Mrs Larkin comes out of the kitchen. 4. He says that he works in a bank. 5. She is making the evening meal. 6. Brutus is the dog owned by the Larkins; he is a Rottweiler.

Übung 3: 1. our 2. furniture 3. friend 4. pie 5. case 6. yard 7. settee 8. Rolex

Übung 4: 1. kitchen 2. ferry 3. train 4. yard 5. shot 6. night

Übung 5: 1. fried egg 2. mushroom 3. add 4. gun 5. tray 6. complain 7. tidy

Übung 6: 1. breakfast 2. suspicious 3. everyone 4. agrees 5. enjoy 6. beautiful 7. laughs 8. father

Übung 7: 1. are 2. eat 3. talk 4. speak 5. appears 6. serve 7. tell 8. have eaten 9. decide 10. sit 11. drink 12. is 13. watch 14. disappear

Übung 8: 1. thirty minutes 2. sounds 3. owl 4. go back 5. quiet 6. barn 7. van 8. seconds 9. Probably

Übung 9: 1. yard 2. light 3. moment 4. hear 5. quietly 6. window 7. cleaner 8. against

Übung 10: 1. eyes 2. barn 3. cloth 4. window 5. floor 6. van

Übung 11: 1. began 2. tied 3. shot 4. looked 5. said 6. did 7. came 8. pushed 9. saw 10. had 11. put 12. knew

Übung 12: 1. cannot 2. at 3. her 4. in 5. barking 6. opens 7. no 8. Will

Übung 13: 1. surprised 2. complain 3. drum 4. injure 5. grubby 6. barn 7. unpack 8. eventually 9. ponytail Lösung: immigrant

Übung 14: 1. mouth 2. daughter 3. discussing 4. inspector 5. answers 6. guns

Übung 15: 1. luck 2. happiness 3. silence 4. danger 5. surprise 6. anger 7. darkness

Stolen Summer

Übung 1: 1. Felder 2. Dorf 3. mitfühlend 4. alt 5. Häuschen 6. Rand 7. geschehen 8. Abend 9. Pforte 10. Gemälde

Übung 2: 1. b 2. c 3. b

Übung 3: 1. Time 2. stop 3. happier 4. nothing 5. church hall 6. noise

Übung 4: 1. Where 2. What 3. When 4. Which 5. Why 6. Who

Übung 5: 1. started 2. to joke 3. looked 4. was talking 5. asked 6. chatted 7. seem 8. seemed 9. wanted 10. to hunt 11. interested 12. playing

Übung 6: 1. e 2. c 3. f 4. h 5. a 6. g 7. i 8. d 9. b
Übung 7: 1. decided 2. were 3. left 4. showed 5. was 6. stopped 7. felt 8. picked
Übung 8: 1. look 2. cook 3. torchlight 4. pretty 5. interesting 6. murderer 7. sell 8. box 9. museum 10. soldier 11. ghost 12. clue
Übung 9: 1. nearby 2. large 3. lots of 4. lovely 5. elderly 6. looked 7. happy
Übung 10: 1. decided 2. had 3. thinking 4. wondering 5. by 6. wanted 7. kept 8. took 9. left 10. know
Übung 11: 1. She 2. They 3. We 4. He 5. them 6. us 7. her 8. him
Übung 12: 1. search 2. reason 3. checked 4. neither of 5. anywhere 6. anything 7. parents
Übung 13: 1. thieves 2. women 3. galleries 4. information 5. memories 6. noises 7. systems 8. witches 9. torches 10. robberies

Death Wish

Übung 1: 1. falsch 2. richtig 3. falsch 4. falsch 5. richtig 6. falsch 7. richtig 8. richtig
Übung 2: 1. evidence 2. madman 3. tension 4. stick 5. important 6. receive 7. victim 8. attempt 9. immediately 10. envelope
Übung 3: 1. children 2. door 3. think 4. mood 5. emotion 6. building site
Übung 4: 1. glue 2. sheet 3. gloves 4. envelope 5. desk 6. stamp
Übung 5: 1. work 2. money 3. children 4. unhappy 5. course 6. need 7. earn 8. answered 9. stand 10. education
Übung 6: 1. can 2. tell 3. happened 4. start 5. got up 6. continues 7. indicates 8. will take 9. will go 10. write
Übung 7: 1. He has received three threatening letters. 2. The postman brings the letters to the house. 3. He should get up early to avoid the traffic. 4. DI Rush has been in the police for 25 years. 5. He has given them a list of names. 6. She wants it because her car will not start.
Übung 8: 1. postman 2. teacher 3. builder 4. policeman 5. joiner 6. butcher 7. housewife
Übung 9: 1. speaks 2. office 3. murder 4. knocks 5. receptionist 6. desk 7. inspector
Übung 10: 1. arrive 2. kitchen 3. wound 4. doctor 5. knife 6. struggle 7. dead
Übung 11: 1. hospital 2. face 3. builder 4. death 5. policeman 6. police station
Übung 12: 1. nodded 2. died 3. thought 4. saw 5. told 6. shut 7. found 8. examined 9. took 10. could
Übung 13: 1. sits 2. works 3. collected 4. reading 5. heard 6. sold

Übung 14: 1. Mr Hanson is going to emigrate to Brazil. 2. The police found a letter in Wise's pocket. 3. The police check the mobile phone of the murdered man. 4. The inspector wants to arrest Hanson.
Übung 15: 1. answer 2. kill 3. remove 4. protect 5. handle 6. emigrate

Motive for Murder
Übung 1: 1. rang 2. came 3. felt 4. found 5. knew 6. left 7. made 8. stood
Übung 2: 1. Everything 2. station 3. desk 4. minutes 5. thank you 6. feeling 7. officers
Übung 3: 1. taken 2. needed 3. everyone 4. found 5. everything
Übung 4: 1. motive 2. suspect 3. funeral 4. death 5. witness 6. threaten 7. secret 8. affair Lösung: murderer
Übung 5: 1. through 2. university 3. appointment 4. with 5. shocked 6. two
Übung 6: 1. She asked Martin about the secret information. 2. They met in a café. 3. She hoped to get a current affairs show. 4. She found it in Tessa's bag. 5. She rang Tessa's friend Maura. 6. Bonnie had written the threatening emails.
Übung 7: 1. innocent 2. real 3. guilty 4. prison 5. freed 6. saying
Übung 8: 1. d 2. f 3. e 4. a 5. b 6. c
Übung 9: 1. a 2. b 3. b
Übung 10: 1. dangerous 2. end 3. luxury 4. threaten 5. go 6. straight away
Übung 11: 1. are meeting 2. is catching 3. am thinking 4. are waiting 5. is hitting
Übung 12: 1. about 2. friend 3. nothing 4. truth 5. documents 6. easy 7. computer
Übung 13: 1. crime 2. whisper 3. never 4. unknown 5. unskilled 6. worry
Übung 14: 1. put 2. colleague 3. arresting 4. were taking 5. waiting 6. about 7. turned
Übung 15: 1. richtig 2. falsch 3. richtig 4. richtig 5. falsch

Lösungen Abschlusstest

Übung 1: 1. They have a Rottweiler. 2. He hears a (gun)shot. 3. They visit the cathedral in Canterbury. 4. He cleans the window so that he can see through it. 5. She locks Brutus in her bedroom. 6. They are paid one thousand pounds for each immigrant.
Übung 2: 1. d 2. e 3. f 4. b 5. a 6. c
Übung 3: 1. prisoner 2. wire 3. unconscious 4. roast 5. choice 6. calm Lösung: pistol

Übung 4: 1. heard 2. walked 3. broke 4. drove 5. stole 6. ate 7. happened 8. paid 9. had 10. felt 11. told 12. glowed 13. hit 14. fought 15. did 16. said
Übung 5: 1. burglar 2. to 3. caught 4. tell me 5. like 6. fault 7. fell
Übung 6: 1. She wanted to be a teaching assistant. 2. A can of petrol was under the seat with the bomb. 3. Jack Wise was the main suspect. 4. He hated Hanson because he hadn't paid him for his work. 5. Sally works in a bank. 6. Her life was insured for one million pounds.
Übung 7: 1. sea 2. murderer 3. criminal 4. worried 5. actor 6. unconcious 7. torchlight 8. filing cabinet 9. take 10. beautifully 11. happily 12. admire 13. angry 14. here 15. laugh
Übung 8: 1. evidence 2. knife 3. chest 4. customer 5. fingerprint 6. attempt 7. suspect Lösung: victims
Übung 9: 1. computer 2. start 3. inspector 4. painting 5. murdered 6. beautiful 7. himself 8. cemetery
Übung 10: 1. Geschrei 2. Geschichte 3. Karriere 4. frieren 5. Anrufbeantworter 6. tief 7. Ledertasche 8. sich streiten 9. die Wahrheit sagen 10. in den Fluss fallen
Übung 11: 1. d 2. f 3. e 4. a 5. c 6. g 7. b
Übung 12: 1. feel 2. try 3. begin 4. sit 5. fall 6. put 7. go 8. can 9. speak 10. see

Glossar

fam	umgangssprachlich
fig	bildlich
pl	Plural
v	Verb

add *v*	ergänzen, hinzufügen
admire *v*	bewundern
adult education college	Volkshochschule
affair	Verhältnis, Affäre
after dark	nach Einbruch der Dunkelheit
alert	Alarmbereitschaft
alert *v*	alarmieren
allotment	Schrebergarten
amazing	erstaunlich
among	unter, zwischen
ankle	Knöchel
apart from	außer
apparently	anscheinend
appear *v*	auftauchen, (er)scheinen
approach *v*	näher kommen
archive	Archiv
around the clock	rund um die Uhr
arrest	Festnahme, Haft
arrest *v*	verhaften
art restoration	Gemälderestauration
at once	sofort; gleichzeitig
at stake	auf dem Spiel
attempt	Versuch
auction house	Auktionshaus
avoid *v*	vermeiden
backed-up against	mit dem Rücken zu
background	Hintergrund
bandage	Binde, Bandage
bandaged	verbunden

bar	*hier:* Riegel; Bar
barn	Scheune
bay	Bucht
be (was, been) *v* **about**	*hier:* in der Gegend sein
beat (beat, beaten) *v*	schlagen
beg *v*	um etwas bitten
behaviour	Verhalten
believe *v*	glauben
belt	Gürtel
blow	Schlag
blow (blew, blown) *v* **one's nose**	(sich) die Nase putzen
boot	Kofferraum
brave	mutig
break (broke, broken) *v* **the law** *fig*	das Gesetz brechen
break (broke, broken) *v* **the story** *fig*	eine brisante Nachricht publik machen
breathe *v*	atmen
building site	Baustelle
bullet	Kugel
bureaucracy	Bürokratie
burglary	Einbruch
burgled	bestohlen
burn *v*	brennen
burst	Ausbruch, Explosion
busy	beschäftigt
buzzer	Summer
calm(ly)	ruhig
calm *v* **down**	(sich) beruhigen
candleholder	Kerzenständer
careful(ly)	vorsichtig
caretaker	Hausmeister
carry *v* **out**	wahrmachen
case	Fall
cautiously	vorsichtig

cemetery	Friedhof
chat *v*	sich unterhalten
check *v*	überprüfen
chemistry	Chemie
chest	Brust
Chief Constable	Polizeipräsident(in)
chilling	schrecklich
choice	Wahl
choke *v*	ersticken
claim *v*	behaupten
clatter *v*	klappern
clear *v* **the table**	den Tisch abräumen
cloth	Tuch
clue	Spur
cobbled	mit Kopfsteinpflaster
collaps *v*	zusammenbrechen
community	Gemeinschaft; Gemeinde
company	Gesellschaft; Firma
competition	Wettbewerb
competitor	Konkurrent(in)
complain *v*	sich beklagen
confess *v*	gestehen
confident	selbstsicher
confused	verwirrt
connection	Verbindung
control room	Zentrale
convenient	günstig
convince *v*	überzeugen
cord	*hier:* Kabel; Seil
court	Gericht
crazy	verrückt
crime scene	Tatort
Crimestoppers number	Telefonnummer für sachdienliche Hinweise
curious	neugierig
current	Strömung

current affairs show	Nachrichtenmagazin
customer	Kunde, Kundin
damp	feucht
dangerous	gefährlich
dare	Wagnis, Herausforderung
dart	Pfeil
deal (dealt, dealt) *v* **with**	sich mit etwas beschäftigen, mit etwas zu tun haben
deny *v*	abstreiten
deserve *v*	verdienen
destroy *v*	kaputtmachen
detail	Detail
dial *v*	wählen
disappear *v*	verschwinden
disappoint *v*	enttäuschen
disturb *v*	durcheinander bringen
do (did, done) *v* **someone a favour**	jdm. einen Gefallen tun
doorway	Türöffnung
doubt	Zweifel
drag *v*	schleppen
drawer	Schublade
dressing	Verband
drown *v*	ertrinken
drum	Trommel
earn *v*	verdienen
ecosystem	Ökosystem, Naturhaushalt
edge	Rand
effort	Einsatz
elderly	betagt, ältere(r)
emergency	Notfall
emigrate *v*	auswandern
en suite	mit eigenem Bad
encouragement	Ermutigung
English Channel	Ärmelkanal
enjoyable	vergnüglich

enquiry	Nachforschung
entry phone	Gegensprechanlage
environment	Umwelt
especially	besonders
eventually	schließlich
evidence	Beweis(material)
examine *v*	untersuchen
exclaim *v*	ausrufen
exhibition	Ausstellung
exist *v*	existieren, bestehen
experience	Erlebnis; Erfahrung
explain *v*	erklären
explosives *pl*	Sprengstoff
fairground	Rummelplatz
fasten *v*	befestigen
fault	Schuld, Fehler
ferry	Fähre
fetch *v*	abholen
file	Akte
filing cabinet	Aktenschrank
find (found, found) *v* **someone guilty**	jdn. für schuldig befinden
fingerprint	Fingerabdruck
fireplace	Kamin
flow *v*	fließen
folder	Mappe
forensic	kriminaltechnisch, forensisch
forensic science laboratory	kriminaltechnisches Labor
for sale	zu verkaufen
fried egg	Spiegelei
fright	Schreck
frighten *v*	erschrecken
frightened	ängstlich
funeral	Beerdigung
gasp *v*	nach Luft schnappen; erstaunt sagen

genuine	echt
get (got, got) *v* **away with sth.**	mit etw. davonkommen
get (got, got) *v* **to one's feet**	aufstehen
ghost	Geist
glove	Handschuh
glow	Leuchten
glow *v*	glühen, leuchten
glue	Klebstoff
good timing *fam*	zur rechten Zeit
gorgeous	herrlich, wunderschön
government	Regierung
grab *v*	packen
grave	Grab
graveyard	Friedhof
grim	ernst, verbissen
growl *v*	knurren
grubby	dreckig, schmuddelig
grunt *v*	grunzen
guilty	schuldig
gun	Gewehr
gunshot	Schuss
hall	Flur
handle *v*	behandeln, anfassen
handsome	attraktiv, gutaussehend
hang (hung, hung) *v* **up**	auflegen (Telefon)
hate	Hass
haunt *v*	spuken in
headstones *pl*	Grabsteine
hen party	Junggesellinnenabschied
hide (hid, hidden) *v*	verstecken
hiya *fam*	Hallo, wie geht's (how are you)
home-made	selbst gemacht
honeymoon	Hochzeitsreise
housekeeper	Haushälter(in)
hug *v*	umarmen
hung	*hier:* erhängt; gehangen

hurt (hurt, hurt) *v*	verletzen
ignition	Zündung
imagination	Vorstellung
immediately	sofort
immigrant	Einwanderer, Einwanderin
impatiently	ungeduldig
impolite	unhöflich
impression	Eindruck
in an instant	in einem Augenblick
incident room	Einsatzzentrale
indicate *v*	zeigen
injure *v*	verletzen
innocent	unschuldig
in person	persönlich
insist *v*	beharren
insulting	abwertend
insurance	Versicherung
insurance policy	Versicherungspolice
insure *v*	versichern
intention	Absicht
interrupt *v*	unterbrechen
interview *v*	befragen
investigate *v*	untersuchen
investigation	Untersuchung
involve *v*	einbeziehen, beteiligen
It's none of your business!	Das geht dich nichts an!
jealous(ly)	eifersüchtig
job interview	Vorstellungsgespräch
joiner	Tischler(in)
junk mail	Werbepost
jury	*hier:* Geschworene; Jury
just in time	gerade (noch) rechtzeitig
landscape	Landschaft
leather	Leder
liquid	Flüssigkeit
lounge	Wohnzimmer

madman, madmen *pl*	Irrer
mansion	Villa
meanwhile	in der Zwischenzeit
memory	Erinnerung
mood	Laune, Stimmung
mortuary	Leichenhalle
motive	Motiv
movement	Bewegung
mud	Schlamm
mumble *v*	murmeln
murder	Mord
murderer	Mörder(in)
mushroom	Pilz
nearby	in der Nähe
nervous(ly)	nervös
news anchor	Nachrichtenmoderator(in)
obsessed	besessen
obtain *v*	erhalten, erwerben
obviously	offensichtlich
off balance	aus dem Gleichgewicht
offer	Angebot
offer *v*	anbieten
old-fashioned	altmodisch
old people's home	Seniorenwohnheim
on fire	in Flammen
opportunity	Gelegenheit
ornament	Schmuckgegenstand
overpower *v*	überwältigen
owl	Eule
pale	blass
paramedic	Sanitäter(in)
pebble	Kiesel
pedestrian	Fußgänger(in)
permission	Erlaubnis
pile	Stapel
plead *v*	bitten, flehen

pleasant	erfreulich
pleased	erfreut
poached	pochiert
poacher	Wilderer, Wilderin
point *v*	richten, zeigen auf
ponytail	Pferdeschwanz
pool	*hier:* Lache; Teich
pottery	Tonware, Keramik
pour *v*	eingießen
presumably	vermutlich
previous	vorig, davor
prison	Gefängnis
prisoner	Gefangene(r)
processing plant	Weiterverarbeitungsanlage
proof	Beweis
protect *v*	schützen
protection	Schutz
proudly	stolz
purr *v*	schnurren
quarry	Steinbruch
rabbit	Kaninchen
reason	Grund
receive *v*	bekommen, erhalten
reception	Empfang
receptionist	Empfangsdame
recognize *v*	(wieder-)erkennen
redden *v*	rot werden
reduce *v*	einschränken, verringern
refreshed	erfrischt; erholt
relationship	Beziehung
relieved	erleichtert
reluctantly	widerwillig
remark *v*	bemerken
remember *v*	erinnern
remove *v*	entfernen
request	Wunsch

research	Forschung
research *v*	forschen
result	Ergebnis
revenge	Rache
(be/get) rid of	los (sein/werden)
right away	sofort
riverbank	Ufer
roast	gebraten
run (ran, run) *v* **(a company/business)**	(ein Geschäft) führen/leiten
rush	Eile
rush *v*	sich beeilen
safety	Sicherheit
sarcastically	sarkastisch
satisfaction	Genugtuung
scapegoat	Sündenbock
scarf	Schal
scientist	Wissenschaftler(in)
scowl *v*	ein böses Gesicht machen
scream	Schrei
scream *v*	schreien
sculptor	Bildhauer
sculpture	Skulptur, Plastik
search warrant	Durchsuchungsbefehl
security camera	Überwachungskamera
serious(ly)	ernst
set (set, set) *v*	stellen; untergehen (Sonne)
set (set, set) *v* **off**	losgehen
settee	Sofa
shake (shook, shaken) *v*	zittern; schütteln
shape	Form
sharp(ly)	scharf; stechend
shift	Schicht
shock	Schock
shocked	schockiert, erschüttert
short-sleeved	kurzärmelig

shrug *v* **one's shoulders**	die Achseln zucken
sigh *v*	seufzen
silence	Stille
sirens *pl*	Sirenen
slam *v*	zuschlagen
slash *v*	aufschlitzen, zerfetzen
slaughterhouse	Schlachthof
slide (slid, slid) *v*	gleiten lassen
slightly	etwas, ein wenig
slim	schlank
smash *v*	zerschmettern, zerschlagen
smoke	Rauch
snarl *v*	knurren
sob *v*	schluchzen
soil	Erde
soldier	Soldat(in)
solicitor	Rechtsanwalt, -anwältin
sourly	griesgrämig
spray paint	Sprühfarbe
stab *v*	erstechen
stall	Stand
statement	Aussage
steal (stole, stolen) *v*	stehlen
steep	steil
stick (stuck, stuck) *v*	kleben
stop *v* **by**	vorbeischauen
straight	gerade; direkt
strange(ly)	seltsam
stranger	Fremde(r)
strangle *v*	erwürgen
stretch *v*	sich strecken
strike (struck, struck) *v*	zuschlagen
struggle	Kampf
struggle *v*	kämpfen; sich winden
stubborn	stur
suggest *v*	vorschlagen, nahe legen

suit *v*	passen
suppose *v*	annehmen
surprise	Überraschung
surprise *v*	überraschen
survival	Überleben
suspect	Verdächtige(r)
suspect *v*	verdächtigen
suspicion	Verdacht
suspicious	verdächtig; misstrauisch
swallow *v*	hinunterschlucken
swear (swore, sworn) *v*	fluchen
swing (swung, swung) *v*	schwingen
switch *v* **off**	ausschalten
switch *v* **on**	anschalten
tabby	getigerte Katze
tension	Nervosität, Anspannung
Thank goodness.	Gott sei Dank.
thatched	reetgedeckt
thief	Dieb(in)
think long and hard	etwas reiflich überlegen
threaten *v*	drohen, bedrohen
tidy	ordentlich
tidy *v* **up**	aufräumen
tie *v*	binden
tissue	Papiertuch
torch	Taschenlampe, Fackel
touch *v*	berühren
trail	Spur
tray	Tablett
tremble *v*	zittern
trial	Prozess
trust *v*	vertrauen
tyre	Reifen
uncomfortable	unbequem, unangenehm
unconscious	bewusstlos, ohnmächtig
under arrest	festgenommen

underestimate *v*	unterschätzen
uneven	uneben
unpack *v*	auspacken
upright	aufrecht
upset (upset, upset) *v*	ärgern
upset	erschrocken
van	Lieferwagen
vegetarian	Vegetarier(in)
victim	Opfer
victim counselling	Opferberatung
view	Aussicht; Sicht
wake (woke, woken) *v*	aufwecken
wake (woke, woken) *v* **up**	aufwachen
wallet	Geldbörse
waste *v*	verschwenden
wave *v*	winken
wavy	gewellt
web	Netz
will	*hier:* Testament; Wille
wire	Draht
wiry	drahtig
witch	Hexe
witness	Zeuge, Zeugin
wonder *v*	sich fragen
worry *v*	sich Sorgen machen
wound	Wunde
wrist	Handgelenk
yard	Hof
yawn *v*	gähnen
yell *v*	(an)schreien